Economy Without Walls

ECONOMY WITHOUT WALLS

Managing Local Development in a Restructuring World

Roger E. Hamlin and
Thomas S. Lyons

Foreword by Schun Hagiwara

Westport, Connecticut
London

Library of Congress Cataloging-in-Publication Data

Hamlin, Roger E.
    Economy without walls : managing local development in a
restructuring world / Roger E. Hamlin and Thomas S. Lyons ; foreword
by Schun Hagiwara.
        p.   cm.
    Includes bibliographical references and index.
    ISBN 0–275–95215–0 (alk. paper)
    1. Economic development projects—United States.   2. Local
government—United States.   3. Privatization—United States.
4. Social choice.   I. Lyons, Thomas S.   II. Title.
HC110.E44H35   1996
338.973—dc20   95–40088

British Library Cataloguing in Publication Data is available.

Library of Congress Catalog Card Number: 95–40088
ISBN: 0–275–95215–0

First published in 1996

Praeger Publishers, 88 Post Road West, Westport, CT 06881
An imprint of Greenwood Publishing Group, Inc.

Printed in the United States of America

The paper used in this book complies with the
Permanent Paper Standard issued by the National
Information Standards Organization (Z39.48–1984).

10 9 8 7 6 5 4 3 2 1

Contents

Foreword

In 1991 the City Planning Institute of Japan memorialized its fortieth anniversary and sponsored "Tokyo Seminar '91: Public-Private Partnerships in Urban Development." The seminar aimed at analyzing and evaluating public-private partnerships in urban development during the 1980s from the international perspective.

The concept of public-private partnership in urban development originated in the United States in the late seventies to create a new mechanism of action to resolve serious and diversified socioeconomic problems in urban areas. The success of this new type of collaboration among individuals and organizations in the public and private sectors in the United States has stimulated actors in the urban development field in other nations, including Japan. The concept has been implemented and has materialized in various forms in the several nations discussed in this book. To underscore the usefulness and popularity of the concept in the international urban development field, speakers from the United Kingdom, France, and the United States contributed to the 1991 seminar and the succeeding workshop.

As a speaker at the Tokyo seminar, I spoke about two past research projects on this subject. One was sponsored by Japan's Housing and Urban Development Corporation (HUDC) in 1985, and the other was a joint research project conducted by Michigan State University and HUDC in 1988 and 1989, in which the authors of this book participated and played key roles.

In the middle of the 1980s, when the first research was accomplished, the concept of *Minkatsu* (utilization of private human and capital resources for urban revitalization) was a key word in Japan. This concept has evolved through the strong influence of Reaganism and Thatcherism. The 1985 research project investigated new roles for HUDC in urban development projects in which private-sector actors had begun to play a crucial role. Two publications by the Committee for Economic Development (CED) in the United States, entitled "Public-Private Partnerships in American Cities: Seven Case Studies," and "Public-Private Partnerships: An Opportunity for Urban Communities," served as stimuli for the 1985 research project. The project was joined by real estate developers, whom the authors call "pure private sector," and the "intermediaries," an insurance company and a bank. The objective of the research was timely and the participants were appropriate, but the discussion between the quasipublic sector actor, HUDC, and the private-sector actors was not well engaged. In the traditional relationship between the public and private sectors, the division between the two sectors was much more distinct than it is now.

The second research effort, completed in 1989, was the first comprehensive research in Japan regarding public-private partnerships in urban development in the American sense. As the authors mentioned, Japan has had de facto types of intersectoral partnerships, and many of them have been quite successful. Both the public- and private-sector actors at that time, however, seemed to look for alternative ways and means for achieving such relationships.The research project was joined by public officials of both the central and local governments, development professionals from the private sector and the intermediaries, and scholars from U.S. and Japanese academic institutions. The transfer of technology and knowledge between the two nations, Japan and the United States, was productively done, but the differences between socioeconomic and political systems in the two nations occasionally precluded proper understanding of such tools as tax-increment financing (TIF) on the Japanese side. The research report, however, is still regarded as the leading text on public-private partnerships in Japan. As an example of its influence, the Ministry of Construction has recently promoted the concept of the town management corporation, a new type of third-sector entity, and refers to TIF as an applicable tool for urban redevelopment in limited urban areas in the not-too-distant future.

We are in the era of the borderless world and society. The potential applicability of successful concepts in one region or nation to other regions or nations could be much higher than a decade ago. The HANDS program in Louisville, Kentucky, which is introduced in this book, could be a great lesson for many urban areas, and the case of Sonic City could offer some hints to U.S. urban development professionals. In this regard, *Economy Without Walls* is timely. The book offers an abundance of case studies and tool information, as well as philosophical suggestions for desirable intersectoral partnerships in the coming age that could inspire the actors for urban development in many nations and help them to recognize the necessity of information exchange on this subject.

Dr. Schun Hagiwara, President
Schun Hagiwara and Urban Matrix Research, Inc.
Tokyo, Japan

Acknowledgments

As with any endeavor of this nature, credit for making this book possible goes to a host of people whose insight, hospitality, perseverance, kindness, talent, generosity, and judgment were major contributions. Since it is not possible to individually thank all of these people here, it is hoped that they know that they have our deep gratitude.

There are several individuals and groups to whom we owe special recognition and thanks. We are particularly grateful to our good friend Dr. Shun Hagiwara, who has afforded us, and our students, numerous opportunities to explore public-private partnerships in Japan. Directly or indirectly, we owe all of our knowledge on the Japanese approach to these mechanisms to Shun. We would also like to acknowledge the contributions of Hajime Yokobori, whose boundless energy made our many site visits to projects in the Tokyo area both possible and exciting.

Our thanks, also, to the Korean Planning Association. The KPA arranged project site visits and sponsored two stimulating conferences in Seoul that related to the projects we studied. One was titled "Dynamic Transformation of Societies," and the other," Strategies for Korean West Coast Development." These greatly influenced our work.

We extend our gratitude to Dr. Robert J. Calcaterra, president of the Arizona Technology Incubator in Scottsdale, Arizona, and his staff, for providing us with information on their program and the partnership that made it possible. We also thank Dr. John I. Gilderbloom, director of the Housing and Neighborhood Development Services (HANDS) Project in Louisville, Kentucky, and his staff, for opening their files to us, inviting us to meetings and workshops, and providing us with guided tours while we were preparing the chapter on HANDS.

We owe a special debt of gratitude to Sumedha Chhatre of the University of Louisville. In addition to coauthoring chapter 6, she spent countless hours conducting telephone interviews, tracking down details, checking sources, and generally making it possible for us to complete this book.

We would like to thank our families for their unending patience and support.

Finally, we would like to thank our editor, James Dunton, at Praeger Publishers, for his patience and flexibility. As always, it was a pleasure working with him.

Introduction: West Berlin and Other Sectors

Recent years have witnessed a revolution in the way economies work. The world has moved away from centralized governments and economies, toward decentralized governments and market-driven economies. Some have termed this a movement from bureaucracy to entrepreneurship (Farrell 1986). In those nations where a private sector exists, it has become more entrepreneurial. In other countries, a fledgling private sector has emerged. Government is pushed to be more entrepreneurial as well, due to increasing economic and fiscal pressures and opportunities (Hamlin and Lyons 1993).

As the ideological debate between communism and capitalism loses its military importance, the "public vs. private" dichotomy diminishes in emotional significance. While centrally controlled economies pursue market reforms, market economies stimulate lagging communities and industries with public incentives. Just as free trade and multinational organizations blur national boundaries, so third-sector organizations blur the distinction between public and private. While the Berlin Wall falls, the walls between the traditionally defined sectors fall within countries and within communities. A pragmatic, nonideological approach to mixed economic systems is becoming the order of the day. The term *economy without walls* takes on both global and local meaning.

Discussion of the local consequences of this pervasive international tendency is less the dominion of economists and more a subject for interdisciplinary analysis and synthesis. This makes the work both more difficult and more rewarding. Yet a desperate need already exists to understand the effects of an economy without walls on local communities. Deteriorating urban conditions render intolerable the typical lag between the initiation of world trends and an understanding of their implications locally.

Numerous popular terms refer to aspects of this entrepreneurial movement. Several labels and the ideas they represent are limiting or confusing in their meaning. Some are tainted with controversy and carry emotional baggage. In most cases, neither the promoters nor the detractors see their piece as part of the revolution that is under way.

The term *privatization* is one example. It describes activities ranging from selling state-owned factories in Poland to contracting out municipal garbage collection in Peoria. While nearly all forms of privatization belong to the entrepreneurial trend, they represent only a portion of the issue discussed in this book.

Public choice theory implies that the population should have greater choice in using and paying for governmental services. This typically means residents pay a fee for a service rather than have it financed out of general taxation. The approach sometimes forces public agencies to compete for customers and raise their own revenues. While also a part of the entrepreneurial movement, public choice is very different from privatization.

Reinventing government expands on both public-choice, fee-for-service theory and the privatization of local services (Osborne and Gaebler 1992). Advocates of reinventing see governmental agencies competing with private firms and other government agencies for service contracts that provide limited monopolies or franchises for certain areas of local services. Reinventing government is clearly part of the world entrepreneurial movement that affects local communities.

During the 1980s, the term *public-private partnerships* was popular. It primarily described governmental use of incentives to leverage private investment to develop major commercial or industrial projects. Nearly every economic system in the world, from centrally planned to free market, used the strategy. The goal was almost always to promote private physical and economic development in places needing economic rejuvenation. Although important, this term in its narrow usage is only part of the issue discussed in this book.

In every case, the terminologies mentioned above start with a public sector and a private sector, and talks about how they relate to one another. This is a false dichotomy. The reality of the entrepreneurial movement requires a new paradigm. Although they have always existed, since about 1980 there has been an explosion in the number and importance of intermediate-sector organizations and activities. These organizations and activities exist in part to promote the public interest, but must also be sensitive to the need to reward investors for taking risks. While *pure public* and *pure private* represent theoretical ends of a spectrum of entities, intermediate-sector behavior is increasingly becoming the accepted practice.

Some have attempted to define a fourth sector (Hagiwara 1991). While third-sector organizations exist to facilitate the relationship between traditional government and investor interests, grassroots citizen groups provide a different slant on what is the public interest and what is good business. These organizations include neighborhood groups, faith-based community organizations, grassroots interest groups, and ad hoc citizen movements. Some occasionally become involved in sophisticated development activities, and others play an important political role in guiding local policy.

The term *public-private partnerships* is sometimes used more broadly than the project-oriented approach mentioned above. It can refer to a variety of activities in which the public sector, the private sector, and an array of intermediate entities influence one another by becoming partners. *Partnership* continues to be an appropriate word, but it connotes relationships much broader than its legal definition. And *public* and *private* refer to goals (pursuit of the public interest vs. the need to reward investors for taking risks) rather than pure organizational forms. Throughout this book, terms like *public-private partnerships* and *intersectoral partnerships* will be used interchangeably and will refer to this more extensive definition.

When referring to this broader concept, only the imagination limits the methods for carrying out such alliances. The goal and the result of promoting intersectoral interaction have, in many cases, been nothing short of the dynamic transformation of an entire social and economic system, an economy without walls.

To date, the entrepreneurial movement has been treated as a phenomenon that grew out of the Reagan-Thatcher era, a conservative economic policy to be described and, alternately, trumpeted and criticized. This approach continues to be a debate about a fictitious dichotomy. This book maintains that intersectoral partnerships are part of our history as well as of our future. They are a natural and logical response to the changing world economy. They present an opportunity to solve many of the problems presented by rapid, large-scale economic change, and often address these at the local level, where they typically arise.

Interaction between sectors also presents challenges to our existing system of ethics and politics, and to our ability to achieve economic and social equity. These latter challenges should not convince us that the concept is fatally flawed and unworthy of serious consideration as a policy tool.

Instead, they should stimulate us to rethink old paradigms regarding the relationships among the various groups that make up our global society.

The purpose of this book is to synthesize our understanding of an economy without walls, distill its implications for local communities, and apply that knowledge to guiding their development. The book assumes that the use of intersectoral partnerships is an important part of any urban and regional development strategy. It attempts systematically to describe such partnerships, including the philosophical foundations of this approach and the financial and nonfinancial activities used to implement it. The book then discusses trends in the theory and practice of local community management that result form this economic restructuring.

The first chapter provides background to the interaction among the public, private, and nonprofit sectors of the economy. The second chapter offers our definition of the term *economy without walls*. It outlines the philosophical and theoretical tenets that surround the use of mixed-venture arrangements. Instead of saying, "Let's do it because it works," the chapter illuminates why and how it works, and what to watch out for. Chapter 3 extrapolates that theoretical foundation to urban and regional development. It gives meaning to the definition at the local or subnational level.

The fourth chapter discusses organizational and legal structures that make such interactions possible. This leads to consideration of specific activities or strategies that can be used to implement urban and regional plans and policies. In each case, how public and private actors are linked to promote private profit and public purpose is carefully described.

Chapters 5, 6, and 7 offer details of several actual examples of complex partnerships for local planning and development in the United States and in other countries. Chapter 5 gives a detailed description of one of the most comprehensive intersectoral approaches to central city redevelopment in the United States, and one of the most successful. Chapter 6 looks at the importance and the methods of small business development as an economic development and urban redevelopment tool both in the United States and in Europe. Chapter 7 talks about three examples of collaborative capitalism for urban redevelopment in northeastern Asia.

Chapter 8 focuses more specifically on the local professional. It explores the implications of the trend toward mixed economies for decision theory, ethics, and professional practice in the fields of urban planning, urban development, and municipal management. These implications are far-reaching for the future of urban planners and related professionals. The ninth chapter uncovers the implications of the new trends presented throughout the book for planning information systems and methods of analysis.

The final chapter provides a summary and draws preliminary conclusions. It attempts to outline an action and research agenda for urban planning, economic development, and municipal management professionals.

The scope of the book is not limited to the United States. People concerned with local development promotion and control have much to learn from international colleagues. Throughout the book, examples of successes and failures from many countries are presented. This should provide practitioners with a useful application of the contents at the same time that ideas are put in a larger context.

The economy without walls is no longer a curiosity. It is a reality, a phenomenon taking place with or without our individual endorsements, presenting challenges that demand attention while simultaneously offering new approaches to making our communities more livable places. With this book, the authors hope to clarify the concept, describe the ways in which it manifests itself globally and locally, identify opportunities associated with the new order, discuss issues associated with those opportunities, and begin the dialogue that can lead to their resolution.

The implications of an economy without walls cannot be ignored if urban planners and related professionals are to be effective in the new worldwide environment.

CHAPTER 1

Background: Necessity
Is the Mother of Invention

THE SHIFTING WORLD ECONOMIC ORDER

From the time of its founding in the late eighteenth century through the nineteenth century, the political economy of the United States could be described as capitalistic, with a laissez-faire attitude toward government. This served the nation well through its largely agrarian beginnings and made the tremendous economic growth of the industrial revolution possible. By the latter decades of the nineteenth century, it became evident that uncontrolled economic growth was causing the overcrowding, poor sanitation, blight, and general squalor plaguing American cities. That a policy of laissez-faire would not solve these problems was also clear.

This realization led the United States toward a major urban reform movement that created the public sector we know today. The backlash against the social transgressions of the nineteenth-century "captains of industry" was so strong that the private sector has never again enjoyed the dominance it did in this nation's first century. As the twentieth century progressed, the public sector, particularly the federal government, assumed a greater role for sustaining the vitality of communities. Increasingly the relationship between the public and private sectors became adversarial.

Strong reliance on the federal government for assistance in effecting the renewal of urban areas derived its impetus from the urban programs of the Roosevelt administration's New Deal of the 1930s and 1940s. It continued with the urban renewal programs of the 1940s, through Lyndon Johnson's

Great Society programs of the 1960s, and the community development block grant and revenue-sharing programs of the Nixon era. Funds from these programs cleared slums, upgraded the built environment, improved public infrastructure, and created jobs for the cities' unemployed (Lyons and Hamlin 1991).

The 1980s saw the pendulum of political attitudes swing again in the direction of laissez-faire. Although unbridled corporate power did not approach that of the previous century, the movement was worldwide. Perhaps in response to the dating of Orwell's classic book *1984*, efforts to reduce the power of government gained political success. The era of Reagan, Thatcher, and Nakasone commenced. In the United States this meant budget cuts, tax cuts, and deregulation. In Great Britain privatization was the order of the day. Japan privatized Nippon Telephone and Telegraph (NTT), creating the largest corporation in the world, and JNR (Japan National Railway) became JR. In the third world, Chile and other nations sought economic takeoff through dramatic deregulation and privatization.

While Western taxpayers were rebelling, antiestablishment ferment was brewing in Eastern Europe and the former Soviet Union. There, we have subsequently seen privatization of public enterprises and public functions on the grandest scale in world history. In Hungary, an early leader in Eastern European privatization, not only were major industrial activities sold but nearly all state-owned property was turned over to local municipalities to "dispose of."

During this period, the diminution of national government power and resources meant a decline in funds for local infrastructure and redevelopment efforts. People who call for a reduction in national power view themselves as lashing out against faceless bureaucrats in a faraway capital city. Only after the fact do they make the connection to the growing pothole in front of their house. Yet, national leaders guarding their own power often cut local allocations first.

In a federal or decentralized system such as the United States, the response to a shortfall in national revenues was to decrease aid to states and localities. In addition to changes in funding, older central cities have experienced the departure of private firms because of structural changes in the national economy. These cities must cope with social and economic problems while their tax bases decline. In Hungary, with its dramatic constitutional decentralization of power in 1992, publicly owned property is now being sold by localities to make ends meet, and local officials are decrying the constant decline in national allocations to localities.

The environment of the 1980s brought a different order for addressing the revitalization of American cities. Budget cuts in the programs most directly affecting urban areas and a change in the global patterns of economic activity mandated the exploration of new avenues for urban economic development (Weaver and Dennert 1987). More specifically, the "new federalism" of the Reagan administration placed the burden of urban revitalization squarely on the shoulders of the cities (Ledebur 1984). These local entities have become more creative in their search for monies to fill the void left by the federal departure.

One solution to the urban fiscal crisis was to privatize some local services provided by government. This has taken a variety of forms ranging from creating a regulated monopoly to handing over a function to private competition. An example of a regulated monopoly is the contracting out of garbage collection to a private firm based on cost and quality proposals. With respect to solid waste or refuse collection, some home owners and businesses have been told by their municipality to choose a collector from a list of firms.

Functions that are not privatized are often turned over to government enterprises. Their managers are told to make ends meet without "subsidy" from general taxation. In the United States, fees have been the fastest-growing category of local revenues.

URBAN REDEVELOPMENT

The decline of the central city has been a world trend. Most cities have experienced a decline of portions of their central cores. Shifting economic patterns, technological innovation, and accompanying residential shifts contribute. The decline has manifested itself in pockets of vacant or under-utilized land; abandoned residential, commercial, and industrial buildings; diminished public infrastructure; population loss; and resultant social problems. The activity directed at revitalizing these underutilized sections of our metropolitan areas has come to be known as urban redevelopment.

City governments throughout the world must now attract private involvement and capital in the solution of problems previously within the exclusive purview of the public sector. This alliance is one form of public-private partnership.

Public development offices are increasingly innovative in their use of the concept, and private-sector actors are more comfortable working in such mixed economic systems. Innovative thinkers in both sectors have conjured up mechanisms for promoting the accomplishment of public policy while compensating investors. We can implement public plans by selectively rewarding entrepreneurs for risking their personal and financial capital. This process has brought greater innovation to government and a greater sense of enlightened self-interest to business.

The United States and Japan are two developed nations that are experiencing surprisingly similar central city problems and are attempting to mitigate those problems via urban redevelopment. Redevelopment efforts in the United States are well documented; the Japanese experience is less widely known. While the authors do not pretend to fully understand Japanese urban history, clearly some of the same forces impinging upon U.S. communities affect Japanese cities. Increasing wage levels and a more technologically oriented, value-added economic structure have changed medium-sized, older industrial cities. In the largest cities, high land values have made housing less feasible in the central core and have forced the population outward.

Japanese professionals perceive that they lag behind the United States in the implementation of public-private partnership for urban redevelopment. Much of the redevelopment activity currently taking place in Japan resembles the project-oriented urban renewal program of the 1950s and 1960s in the United States. Emphasis is on governmental involvement in acquisition and assembly of land for private development. Highly sophisticated mechanisms have evolved to deal with land problems.

Several probable reasons exist for Japan's unique entrance into this arena. First is the position of government in Japan. Japanese society holds the public sector, and the upper-level civil servants in it, in very high esteem. Society does not perceive government as handmaiden to private enterprise, and therefore, the private sector holds no such expectations. Second, population density is very high in Japan. This exacerbates another problem: physical urban infrastructure is difficult to improve. Streets are narrow, making the provision of utilities more expensive. Third, land ownership is revered. Individual parcels are passed down through families for centuries. Fourth, land is expensive. Fifth, land transfers incur a high capital gains tax.

These factors focus city redevelopment on the problems of assembling land, tearing down existing buildings and structures, improving infrastructure, and property improvements. It is in addressing these problems that public-private partnership has its greatest present and future value to Japan. The government and private developers can accomplish much together in the way of assembling small parcels and providing adequate infrastructure. Since the landowner's greatest concern is the heavy burden of property and capital gains taxes, the government can help to encourage development and redevelopment by providing ways to lighten this burden.

Given these realities of Japanese urban development, it is not surprising to find that most public-private partnership—and most planning in Japan, for that matter—is project-oriented. The major public-private actor is the Housing and Urban Development Corporation (HUDC). This entity is a public authority that behaves like a private company. It is the descendant of Japan's post–World War II Housing Authority.

The HUDC raises money for its development activities by selling bonds to individuals in the marketplace. It defines a redevelopment project area and uses the money generated by bond sales to purchase the land, clear it, readjust property lines, rebuild, or sell or lease the land to private developers. Because of the nature of landownership in Japan, HUDC may have to negotiate for ten to fifteen years to acquire a project area. HUDC has the power of eminent domain, but seldom uses it because Japan is a society of consensus and not of law.

The Republic of Korea, caught in time between the developing world and the older developed economies, is facing some of the urban problems of both. It, too, uses complex intersectoral processes for land assembly, finance, and development. The Korean Land Development Corporation (KLDC) is a third-sector organization comparable with Japan's HUDC. It works with private developers to tackle problems from inner city redevelopment to creation of satellite cities. Bundang New Town, one of its largest projects, has a population of 500,000.

Eastern European countries may represent the most unusual and illustrative examples of economy without walls. They are starting from scratch. Since they have lived with very little private sector for decades, they have fewer preconceived notions about the distinctions between public and private. In Hungary, the new constitution gave local governments nearly full freedom to act either as a government or as a private enterprise in promoting local economic development. For better or worse, in one pen stroke, they leap-frogged the decades of gradual evolution toward mixed economic systems experienced in the United States.

The term *public-private partnerships* has been popular since about 1980, and has taken on a broader meaning and new importance. Many activities described in this book have been common for decades, and some are fundamental to the workings of any system of development.

Most of the formal discussion about such partnerships focuses on nations of the industrialized world, but emerging nations are engaging in relevant, innovative efforts not labeled *public-private partnerships*. They often promote the nonformal sector, cooperatives, and self-help projects, even when the economy is under strong central control. Because legal systems are often less solidified and bureaucratized than in Western industrialized countries, a form of entrepreneurship prevails in the daily lives of all citizens.

CHAPTER *2*

Philosophical and Conceptual Foundations: Why Walls Must Go

To discuss the complex subject of intersectoral partnerships in worldwide urban development, we must define terms precisely, so as to proceed with a common vocabulary. We start by defining *economy without walls* and *public-private partnerships*.

By *economy without walls* we mean a society in which a high percentage of formal and informal organizations cannot be identified with either the public sector or the private sector. While the public interest is identified and sought, and while investor risk is respected and rewarded, public and private goals are often pursued simultaneously within organizations and through alliances of organizations. The economy's actors are increasingly found on a spectrum of intermediate entities. The term *economy without walls* is chosen to emphasize the dramatic change this represents for society by analogy to the powerful effect of the crumbling of the walls of the Iron Curtain.

Numerous attempts have been made to define intersectoral partnership. Definitions of *public-private partnerships* from the early 1980s continue to serve. It has been labeled *third-party government*, and some have called it *neocorporatism* (Weaver and Dennert 1987). The most complete definition comes from the Committee for Economic Development in the United States (CED):

Public-private partnership means cooperation among individuals and organizations in the public and private sectors for mutual benefit. Such cooperation has two dimensions: the policy dimension, in which the goals of the community are articulated, and the operational dimension, in which those goals are pursued. The purpose of public-private partnership is to link these dimensions in such a way that the participants contribute to the benefit of the broader community while promoting their own individual or organizational interests. (Holland 1984, 210)

It should be clear from this definition that intersectoral collaborations are not just organizational arrangements, but also processes. The partnership process involves all interactions between public, private, and intermediate-sector actors, including establishing structures and using those structures to achieve mutual benefit. The idea lends itself well to the planning process, in that it brings together the principal players in urban policy formulation and implementation. Indeed, when this process carries the label "strategic planning," public-private partnership is considered essential to its success (Sorkin, Ferris, and Hudak 1986). The fact that the partnership arrangement attempts to balance self-interest with the public interest makes it all the more attractive in a democratic society (though it complicates the achievement of equitable representation).

We must also ask, What is development? What does development require? What unique characteristics does urban development have? When these are answered, we can proceed to talk about how intersectoral partnerships promote development. In this chapter the first two of these questions will be explored.

Summarily defined, *development* means increasing a population's ability to acquire a higher standard of living (Hamlin and Lyons 1993). This brief definition does not presuppose one's definition of a higher standard of living, nor does it impose a methodology for acquiring it. For purposes of this book, *urban development* focuses on physical development as a means of achieving other economic and social ends. However, it can refer to more abstract improvements in quality of life.

The next question is How does development take place? More basically, What are the prerequisites for achieving a higher standard of living? While not all improvements in standard of living can be described in monetary or financial terms, they are all economic. Using the parlance of the economist, we suggest six prerequisites for development to occur: surplus, savings, investment, stability, efficiency, and equity. Each of these basic economic issues, shown in Table 1, will now be looked at in detail, with an eye toward the meaning of intersectoral partnerships (Hamlin and Lyons 1993).

SURPLUS

Surplus means that goods and services available in a society exceed the amount necessary for subsistence-level consumption. Clearly, wealthy so-

Table 1
The Six Prerequisites for Development

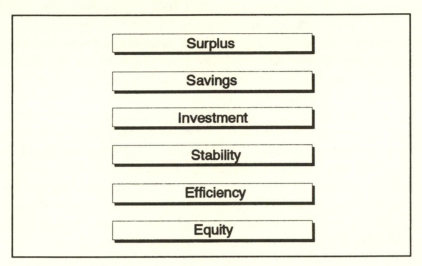

Surplus

Savings

Investment

Stability

Efficiency

Equity

cieties have more surplus than do the not so wealthy, but this disparity can be overstated. Nearly every society and community can generate a surplus, and the surplus of less-developed nations is typically underestimated. Furthermore, the use that is made of a surplus may be more important than its amount.

One should always view the surplus as surplus time and talent, rather than excess money or physical product. Excess physical product can be converted to time by ceasing production of the surplus commodity. This time can be consumed as free time, or can be redirected toward the production of non-subsistence goods and services. A person's time and accompanying talents are the common denominator, not rice in the storage bins or money in the bank.

Even if a society is near subsistence, it may not be fully utilizing idle time. Less economically developed societies typically have substantial unemployed human resources. Nations of Eastern Europe and the former Soviet Union have vast amounts of underemployed talent. A surplus of idle time and talent throughout society cannot be saved. Human time is a perishable resource that disappears if not used. The public sector may need to play a partnership role in promoting the utilization of that surplus, by productively employing labor or stimulating economic growth (Hamlin and Lyons 1993).

SAVINGS

Savings means that surplus accumulates. Individuals defer enjoyment of their surplus until another time. Industrialized countries measure savings monetarily. What is really being saved in any society is the human time and effort necessary to create the saved surplus. Savings can take the form of nonperishable commodities, monetary representations of those commodities, or a promise to repay time in the future.

The portion of the surplus that is saved is crucial. No economic development can take place without savings. For a developing society, the more savings, the better. In a market-oriented economy, the level of savings is up to each individual. Centrally planned economies force savings through taxation or government ownership. Mixed economies have some of both. One axiom about saving is clear: government can never force adequate sustained savings. When it tries through public ownership or heavy taxation, it reduces the incentive to utilize time and destroys the surplus.

Government must induce savings through a reward system strong enough to convince people to defer some of their present enjoyment into the future. The only way to induce savings is to make saving enjoyable in the present. Society achieves this when people envision the satisfaction they may gain in the future, or when individuals receive an immediate, indirect benefit from saving, such as higher social status. In cultures where people cannot imagine the future or where status comes from displaying wealth rather than accumulating it, long-term improvements in the quality of life cannot take place.

Governments can induce savings only by changing the cultural basis for saving. They may achieve this through strong financial and psychological inducements, such as appealing to patriotism or promising higher community status for savers. To create these inducements, an important public-private collaboration is government's partnership with the saver. Since both the individual and the society benefit from high savings rates, both must share in the risks and rewards. Little saving takes place in any society without this partnership, resulting in the stagnation of development.

As the first step in this partnership process, government must ensure that the chance of losing one's savings does not exceed the risk the saver is willing to take or the reward the saver can receive. Long-term societal stability is a key ingredient in that chemistry. Maintaining bank security is another. Insuring deposits is a strategic partnership role that often involves the government, a quasigovernmental insurance corporation, the savings, and the saver. The savings institution may be a for-profit shareholder corporation, a mutual institution, or a cooperative such as a credit union.

The second step is recognizing the key ingredients of the psychological inducement to save. In some societies, the home is the most important long-term reservoir of personal wealth. In such cultures, insuring the security of the home and promoting home ownership may be the primary mechanisms for inducing savings. In other cultures, the same might be said about the extended family's compound. In a village-based culture, improvements in the village's infrastructure may be the best reservoir of savings. In still other societies, saving for old age security is a primary inducement to setting aside part of the surplus. In those cultures, governmental involvement to maintain the integrity of retirement plans can be a strong force for promoting needed savings. Buying insurance represents a form of savings in societies keen on reducing future uncertainty. In each example mentioned above—home ownership, community infrastructure, retirement systems, and insurance—carefully crafted and balanced partnerships between government, private, and intermediate-sector institutions are critical.

As the third step in the public's partnership with the saver, government must establish mechanisms to promote broad-based savings, not just saving by the wealthy. For example, savings accounts are often the only form of monetary savings available to the average citizen of a developing country. If currency inflation undermines the real value of local bank deposits, it destroys the incentive for monetary savings. Only those wealthy enough to buy large-denomination, international financial instruments will be induced to save. The societal benefit of that savings often flows to another country (Hamlin and Lyons 1990).

INVESTMENT

An individual can save time and store it in a variety of monetary and nonmonetary forms. Yet, as indicated above, time is perishable. Development requires the immediate translation of some savings into investment. Saved time and talents are then used to create more efficient production methods, producing more surplus in the future. Investment can take the form of new tools, processes, knowledge, education, or training. The translation of savings into investment demands strong intermediary organizations. These intermediaries are go-betweens or brokers. They effectively link the saver with the appropriate kind of investment.

A society must possess a variety of investment vehicles to match different saving and investment needs. Some must serve high-risk endeavors while others rent surplus time to lower-risk activities. Some investment vehicles provide equity capital (i.e., rent time in exchange for ownership or control).

Others offer debt capital, a return on investment without ownership and control. Some investments must be available for the long term, whereas other investments need only assume risk for a short time (Hamlin and Lyons 1993).

The financial intermediary system should translate savings into investments in varying magnitudes, ranging from billions of dollars to promote heavy industrial and technological development, to a few hundred dollars for small enterprise creation. Investment vehicles should be available for both collateralized and noncollateralized transactions. The intermediary system should be capable of channeling surplus into human investment, such as education and training, as well as into capital assets, such as buildings, machinery, and equipment. The system must be able to focus savings on both public infrastructure and private assets (Hamlin and Lyons 1993).

Most modern intermediaries are financial, such as banks, stock markets, and insurance companies. Nonfinancial intermediaries must also be present. Maintaining a nonmonetized mechanism for translating savings into investment is particularly important in a less economically developed society because the surplus of time is less monetized. An example of such an intermediary is a housing cooperative. Here, members contribute time to build a house for a neighbor with the promise of reciprocation in the future. This mechanism effectively employs a surplus resource (time), promotes savings (a promise to receive benefit in the future), and instantly channels savings into investment in social overhead capital (housing) (Hamlin and Lyons 1993).

Intermediaries represent the essence of intersectoral synergy, balancing the public interest with a need to reward savings and risk. Without a partnership with public involvement, adequate intermediaries would not exist. They would not occur to the degree or in the variety necessary for the full array of economic activity to flourish. Even in highly advanced industrialized societies, such as Japan, Singapore, and the United States, the variety of intermediaries is often inadequate. In one culture, large corporations may have no trouble raising capital, whereas small business development stagnates. In another country, both low-risk capital and venture capital may be abundant, but intermediate-risk seed capital remains nonexistent (Hamlin and Lyons 1990). In Eastern Europe, recognition of the partnership aspect of intermediaries has been a key determinant of a society's success in making the transition to a market economy.

Highly industrialized societies seem to lose their capacity to maintain nonmonetized intermediary systems. Economically advanced nations are just now learning the potential that public-private partnerships offer for translating savings into investment in this way. In some cases, they are learning techniques from developing nations and applying them to economically depressed zones (Hamlin and Lyons 1990). Perhaps nations of the former Soviet Union should look to the developing world rather than the West for advice about how to employ idle time and talent by using nonmonetary intermediaries.

Some ways in which government acts as a partner with the intermediary systems are (1) to maintain a stable monetary system so as to monetize the intermediary process; (2) to regulate financial intermediaries; (3) to create a central financial intermediary that acts as the banker's banker; (4) to share risk by insuring deposits; (5) to legally sanction an array of intermediary organizations to serve the variety of intermediary needs described above; and (6) to invest its own surplus selectively in private-sector activities to induce private entities to behave in ways that promote public policy goals. Items (5) and (6) require further elaboration.

With respect to (5), some intermediaries are common and seem obvious. They include banks, stock markets, bond markets, and pension funds. Alone, these traditional vehicles leave huge gaps in the continuum of investment needs. Venture capital, seed capital, and pre-venture capital organizations must also be present. Loan insurance pools allow for medium-risk loans not provided by traditional banks. Mutual funds allow the very small saver to acquire corporate ownership. Also, public-purpose, nonprofit organizations induce and channel contributed wealth. Real estate investment trusts allow the small investor to participate in real estate ownership. The creation of secondary mortgage markets gives the small saver a vehicle by which to become a provider of mortgage financing (Hamlin and Lyons 1990).

Concerning (6), selective investment of public funds, numerous options have become available. Quasigovernmental organizations are now providing direct loans to private companies and offering subordinated loans that reduce bank risk and induce bank participation in partnership with the public. They are also purchasing loans in secondary markets to inject funds into banks (Flick 1987). Both national and local governments are participating in equity capital by purchasing stock, stock options, royalty agreements, or warrants, or entering into formal partnership arrangements. Third-sector organizations may stimulate equity investment indirectly by giving low-interest loans to venture capital and pre-venture capital companies. Governments also give grants that must be matched by private investment. Government's role is not to become the source of capital but to be a catalyst for increased private savings and investment.

STABILITY

Stability means that events such as political upheaval will not destroy the surplus, the savings, or the investment. As with many issues, perceptions are more important than reality. Perhaps better said, the general perception of the population is its own reality. The perception of instability is nearly self-fulfilling. If people view a situation as unstable, they will not have an incentive to save or invest. Economic growth will stagnate, and political and economic instability will ensue. In an urban setting, stability takes on a spatial context. If a city or neighborhood is perceived as unstable, investment will quickly flow elsewhere (Hamlin and Lyons 1993). In addition to government's obvious role in maintaining political stability, intersectoral partnerships are critical to returning a sense of social, economic, and political stability to declining neighborhoods or regions before the development process will continue there.

EFFICIENCY

Efficiency means the allocation of resources, goods, and services where they produce the greatest improvement in standard of living per unit of input. Common sense might suggest that a central authority could scientifically allocate resources. Yet the appropriate allocation varies from day to day, with people's needs and desires. This phenomenon is far too rapid and complex for any central bureaucracy to cope with. If the public sector attempts to control too much of the allocation process, it hinders efficiency. Marketplaces aid the ability of the allocation process to respond quickly to changes in human desires, but maintaining effective markets requires a partnership between the public and private.

EQUITY

Equity is also a prerequisite of development. If the gap between income groups becomes too large, or if people feel the system is unfair, trust breaks down and instability ensues. People will not save or invest, and democratic institutions become dominated by a smaller group, thus exacerbating the lack of trust.

PERFECT COMPETITION

The concept of intersectoral partnerships assumes that in most cases, a free-market system is the best allocator of goods, services, and resources in a society. It is the best expression of people's desires, and of their willing-ness and ability to pay. This implies that it is generally the most appropriate mechanism for facilitating development. Under this assumption, govern-ment should leave to the private sector all activities it can carry out (Lyons and Hamlin 1991).

The term *free competitive market* implies a marketplace that meets certain criteria. If it does not meet them, it is not a good allocator of goods and services. Economists have defined a free competitive market as one that realizes perfect competition. In its ideal state such a market has the follow-ing characteristics:

1. A large number of buyers and sellers participate in the marketplace, and no one has a significant impact on the market.
2. The product sold in the market is highly divisible; in other words, it can be purchased in small individual units.
3. Each unit of product is indistinguishable in quantity and quality.
4. An auction market procedure establishes the price of each unit, based on supply and demand.
5. All buyers and sellers possess perfect knowledge about functioning of the market, including price and quality.
6. No externalized costs or benefits result from behavior of the market participants. (Mahanty 1980).

A model or paradigm expresses an ideal condition that can never fully exist. A sound market that properly allocates goods and services is one that approaches the model of perfect competition. If a market has serious flaws in comparison with the perfect model, it may not be a good allocator of goods and services. It may actually cause distortions and instabilities throughout the economy (Lyons and Hamlin 1991).

JUSTIFICATION FOR GOVERNMENT INVOLVEMENT

Clearly, the provision of some goods and services does not come close to matching the model of perfect competition. Some services, such as police protection, are nearly indivisible. Either they are provided or they are not, and the externalities associated with their provision or lack of provision are enormous. Such goods and services, if demanded by the population, must be supplied by the public sector and their cost must be covered by the public. Other goods and services fit easily into the perfect competition model. They tend to be produced and sold by entrepreneurs, even in the most centralized of economies. Between these two is an array of goods and services that require partnership between the public sector and the private sector, regardless of the ideology of the society (Hamlin and Lyons 1993).

The theory of public choice defines a pure private good as one that can be effectively traded in a pure competitive market, meeting the definition of perfect competition discussed above. Potential consumers can be excluded from the benefit unless they are willing and able to pay the price. In contrast, a pure public good exhibits the opposite characteristics. It is indivisible. Buyers and sellers do not exist in great numbers. No auction market can function; buyers and sellers have little knowledge about the product; externalities abound. Furthermore, consumers cannot be kept from enjoying the benefits. "Once public goods are provided for some, they will be available to others, without reference to who pays the cost" (Ostrom and Ostrom 1971).

Because market imperfections do exist, it sometimes becomes necessary for governments to intervene in the private marketplace. Few would question that assertion, although the appropriate degree of intervention is a matter of debate. The real question is how to intervene effectively (Lyons and Hamlin 1991). One approach is for government to take over a market and provide the goods or services directly. This may be an appropriate solution where market imperfections are overpowering and permanent, where the product is indivisible, economies of scale are large, externalities are prodigious, information is bad or unavailable, and the market becomes monopolistic. The temporary government appropriation of a market might be reasonable in order to establish and stabilize those markets adversely affected by external events. An example might be the direct provision of housing to a nation shattered by war or natural disaster (Lyons and Hamlin 1991).

A second mode is for government to act to perfect the markets. In other words, if market imperfections cause severe dislocations that induce businesses to behave contrary to public policy, discover how the characteristics of that market deviate from the model of perfect competition. Government should then act to bring the behavior of the market closer to the model (Lyons and Hamlin 1991).

To restate this idea, if private markets do not operate efficiently, or do not produce outcomes desired by public policy, then the public sector should carefully use both the carrot and the stick to nudge the private sector in the proper direction. The stick represents laws and regulations that coerce individuals and companies to follow some minimum standard of behavior; the carrot represents incentives for more optimal behavior. These incentives take the form of regulatory relaxation, financial inducements, or coordination. This system of incentives is generally referred to as "public-private partnerships" (Lyons and Hamlin 1991).

CHAPTER *3*

Urban and Regional Development: Where Laissez-Faire Never Worked

When analyzing urban and regional development, one finds that the markets affecting the way cities function and grow are often in a middle ground. They function as private markets, but with numerous imperfections relative to the economist's perfect competition mode (Lyons and Hamlin 1991).

REAL ESTATE MARKETS

Market imperfections are endemic to the urban real estate market. Instead of offering many identical, highly divisible units, this market includes many unique parcels of land. Each has its own locational characteristics, shape, size, and infrastructure services. Locational factors can change rapidly as urban infrastructure is added and traffic patterns change (Lyons and Hamlin 1991).

Typically, participants have poor access to information. Finding out which parcels are on the market is often difficult. To negotiate the price, one needs to contact the owner's representative. Secret negotiations, trades, and special prices are common. The number of buyers for each unique parcel is small, and each seller is nearly a monopolist for that parcel. Externalities abound in the real estate market because the use of one property greatly affects the value of surrounding properties.

Because of the high level of externalities, whenever a district of the city takes on negative physical, social, or economic characteristics, reversing direction becomes difficult. A downward spiral may ensue: market forces become extremely distorted, the perception of stability is lost, and the natural process of urban renewal fails. At some point the public must strongly intervene if it is in the public interest for the neighborhood to survive. This intervention should take the form of strategic intersectoral partnerships with the goal of restoring market conditions. Otherwise, market failure will continue and public-sector intervention will turn into dependency. Chapter 5 describes such a case in Louisville, Kentucky.

Common externalities associated with older or poorer communities include the following:

1. Chaotic subdivision of land, characterized by irrational lot lines, resulting in odd-shaped or small plots that impede parcel assemblage for development.

2. An inadequate infrastructure, which is expensive to repair and/or replace, and discourages economic development when left unattended. Due to fiscal problems, many central cities have deferred maintenance for their public infrastructure, a situation that only exacerbates the problem.

3. The mixing of incompatible uses of land, which ultimately blights the affected area and reduces property values. This situation reduces tax revenues generated by the area, which in turn diminishes the government's ability to provide public services.

4. Social disorganization, such as crime, which reduces the quality of life in a given urban area, drives out middle-class residents and may ultimately disrupt commerce (Lyons and Hamlin, 1991).

Any combination of these factors can make an urban area difficult and prohibitively expensive to renew. To control urban development, prevent decay, and promote the natural process of urban renewal, intersectoral partnerships that perfect markets by mitigating externalities are not just a novel idea but a necessity (Hamlin and Lyons 1989).

Real estate externalities are so complex that success may create public policy problems. An urban district that succeeds in attracting high-rise office structures may become incompatible with residential uses. This may result in the area becoming deserted after working hours. Ensuing social and political problems may cause it to be even less desirable as a residential area, thus producing a downward spiral in district population. High rents drive the population further from their place of employment, increasing the time and money costs of commuting. Concern about this problem in Tokyo is discussed in the Okawabata project case in Chapter 7.

HOUSING MARKET

Many imperfections are unique to the housing sector of the real estate market. Certain segments of the housing market function adequately, but others do not. The housing market for low- and low-middle-income families has not functioned well, in any country, without governmental involvement. Since housing is a necessity, ability to pay segments the market, limiting the number of buyers and sellers in each submarket. Interest rates that affect finance charges influence ability to pay.

Housing markets are also highly localized. Lower-income people face severe locational constraints because of poor transportation to services or industrial jobs. Transportation disadvantagement and the need to be close to work or services force lower-income urban residents to compete for housing in areas of the central city where land costs are high and the housing stock is old. Racial and ethnic discrimination exacerbates market imperfections, reducing housing choice for some groups. These factors sometimes push the market rent for low-quality units higher than for higher-quality housing. Alternatively, in the developing world, market pressures force lower-income people into fringe areas and require them to spend hours commuting to low-paying jobs.

The financial intermediary process also breaks down for lower-income housing. Banks are reluctant to lend to prospective home buyers or apartment developers in neighborhoods perceived to be at risk of decline. A vicious circle of events ensues in which flaws in the market for moderate-cost housing exacerbate other flaws. The free market's ability to supply housing adequately to certain segments of the population degenerates (Lyons and Hamlin 1991).

COPING MECHANISM

Some mechanisms used to overcome these externalities are financial. Essentially the strategy is to use a partnership arrangement both to induce investment and to focus investment in neighborhoods and communities with particular needs (Fosler and Berger 1982). Typically this involves government's sharing the risk associated with investing in redevelopment areas.

Some urban and regional plan implementation strategies involve partnership activities that are not primarily financial. One strategy creates land use control incentives. It relaxes controls when a company or project promotes other public policy goals. Another is to allow for the transfer of air rights and development rights. A third approach calls for government to provide assistance through land acquisition, assembly, and readjustment so as to overcome externalities associated with irrational lot lines. (For a description of land readjustment, see Chapter 4 or Minerbi et al. 1986.) This is a key role for the public side because the public sector can typically use a "taking" power, such as eminent domain, not available to the private sector. Land assembly presents a particularly difficult problem for the private sector, inhibiting urban redevelopment all over the world. Once government purchases the land, it can write down the selling price (sell at a discount) to stimulate development. Concentrating infrastructure improvements in an area targeted for development or redevelopment is another strategy. The public sector also can assist in project feasibility studies because government collects data necessary for such analysis. Targeted labor force training and management training also may be effective (Hamlin and Lyons 1989).

One role of government in urban development is to act as a grand coordinator of large-scale redevelopment projects. This is much like the role increasingly performed by the Housing and Urban Development Corporation in Japan (described in a case study in Chapter 7) or the New York Urban Development Corporation. The quasigovernmental agency can increase communication between market participants, reduce externalities through planning, and increase the value of each parcel through property assemblage, readjustment, and infrastructure improvement. Tax incentives, labor and management training, financial incentives, and the relaxation of development controls might be concentrated in the same area for maximum impact.

Chapter 4 describes and offers examples of these and many other partnership activities. To accomplish this urban development coordination, a number of "in-between" organizational structures can be used. These are described in Chapter 4.

Public–Private Processes: Herman Miller Style

ORGANIZATIONAL STRUCTURES

As stated previously, public-private partnerships are not just organizational structures, but processes to achieve public and private objectives. These strategic collaborations take on several forms and are useful urban revitalization tools in a variety of circumstances. They are sometimes created to address a single development issue or carry out a single project. In other cases, they stand as permanent associations prepared to address ongoing issues within their jurisdictions (Lyons and Hamlin 1991).

To develop an understanding of public-private partnerships, it is useful to explore the forms these processes take, their legal structure, primary sources of funding, and their leadership arrangements. Some may be completely equal partnerships between government and business, while others are largely private organizations with public officials serving on their boards of directors (Levy 1981). Funding for these activities may come from private sources, public sources, membership fees, income earned from development, or from other partnerships (Ahlbrandt and Weaver 1987). The rest of this section is a further examination of the various structures used to facilitate public-private partnerships in the United States and other parts of the world. Table 2 depicts the relationships among several such structures.

Mixed Partnerships

A partnership is "a voluntary contract between two or more competent persons to place their money, effects, labor, and skill, or some or all of them,

Table 2
Major Organizational Structures of Public-Private Partnerships

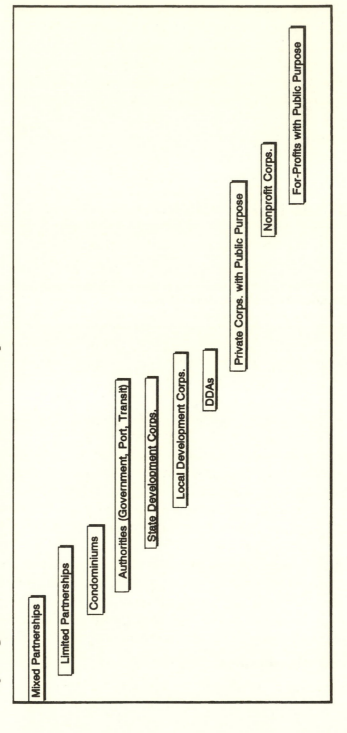

in lawful commerce or business, with the understanding that there shall be a proportional sharing of the profits and losses between them" (Black 1968, 1277). In a legal sense, the term "persons" includes legal organizational entities such as corporations or other partnerships and individual citizens. This legal arrangement has been extrapolated to similar arrangements between public and private organizations. Public organizations such as cities are legally nonprofit corporations and can enter into partnership arrangements. Some intersectoral partnerships are simply legal arrangements in which both the government and private participants maintain their autonomy. They agree to work cooperatively to solve local problems for the benefit of all parties. The contributions of the parties to such a collaboration need not be equal (Lyons and Hamlin 1991).

The public sector, the private sector, and other nonprofit organizations may form either single-purpose or multipurpose mixed partnerships. One mixed partnership may deal solely with marketing or promoting the community. Another may engage in planning, research, and community development (Ahlbrandt and Weaver 1987).

U.S. tax law affords certain advantages to a partnership. Paper losses resulting from declaring real estate depreciation expenses pass through to each partner's tax return, offsetting other real estate profits. Partner liability constitutes the disadvantage of a partnership structure. Liability is not limited, as it is with a corporate structure (Lyons and Hamlin 1991).

In some countries, such as Japan, there is no legal basis for partnerships. Thus, no general or limited partnerships are found. There, "joint ventures" allow collaboration for urban redevelopment.

Limited Partnerships

In a limited partnership, one or more of the legal individuals act as general partners, while the remaining participants act as special (limited) partners. The special partners contribute funds but are not liable for the debts of the partnership beyond this contribution. The general partners manage the funds, select sites, and carry out the actual development effort (Thomsett 1988). For example, the government and a private business may form a limited partnership for the redevelopment of a particular area in the city. The government and the private business are the general partners in this limited partnership. They then sell limited partnership units (shares) to investors who seek an adequate return (Lyons and Hamlin 1991).

If the project can be structured to provide an adequate return on investment, the general partners provide leadership and the limited partners provide equity financing with limited risk. For the general partners the tax advantages and liability disadvantages of a straight partnership pertain (Lyons and Hamlin 1991). Because of the lack of a partnership enabling law, limited partnerships do not exist in Japan.

Mixed Condominiums

Under a condominium arrangement, individuals own distinct physical parts of the development project. As members of an association, they also own other parts of the project in common. The most typical condominium is a multifamily housing complex. Here, members of the association own the interior walls and fixtures of each housing unit privately, while exterior walls, facilities, and grounds are owned in common. Voting power on association matters is often allocated by unit. Alternately, it can be based on the number of square feet owned, the value of each unit, or other factors (Lyons and Hamlin 1991).

A condominium may have commercial, office, industrial, or residential uses. For purposes of this book, an interesting arrangement is where governmental or quasigovernmental entities own some private units. One example is an industrial park organized as a condominium with a government as the owner-developer. This arrangement allows for lot lines to move to fit the needs of the incoming companies without the legal problems associated with replatting.

Another project has an office tower, hotel, underground parking garage, and recreational plaza. The condominium consists of three separate ownership units plus areas owned in common by the three. The three units are the hotel, owned by a national franchise; the office tower, owned by a real estate development firm; and the garage, owned by the city. The common areas consist of the land, the foundation, the plaza, and an atrium between the tower and the hotel. The three unit owners contribute equally to the cost of maintaining the atrium and superstructure, and have equal votes in the association. Because of the size of each ownership unit, the authors call this a mega-condominium (Lyons and Hamlin 1991).

A condominium within a condominium is also possible. One group of units may own some property in common, and this group, as a whole, is a unit in a larger mega-condominium arrangement. This allows for mixed uses in a legal condo arrangement in a planned unit development.

Government Authorities

Semipublic organizations created by government statute or ordinance are typically governmental authorities. Although some are publicly financed, they function independently of state and local governments. Port authorities, transit authorities, and economic development corporations are among their ranks. They possess some of the flexibility of a private corporation while maintaining some of the powers of public entities (Levy 1981). They are especially useful for generating central city development (Lyons and Hamlin 1991).

Port and Transit Authorities

Although their primary function is to provide security, maintenance, and traffic control at seaports, many port authorities have staff that specialize in promoting and facilitating development within their local area (Conway and McKinley 1966). Port authorities promote their facilities to industry (Gilmore 1960), provide information on potential plant locations in their areas, and supply data on tariff rates, transportation schedules, and engineering considerations (Conway and McKinley 1966). Some port authorities plan industrial districts and additional port facilities within their jurisdiction (Gilmore 1960).

Transit authorities participate actively in local development, but to a lesser extent than port authorities. Their development efforts include promoting their jurisdictions to industry and cooperating with businesses in providing service. They offer ridership data to businesses seeking to assess the availability of local labor or the local market for their products and services (Lyons 1987).

State-Level Development Corporations

In the United States, many states have created development authorities. Among these organizations are the Kentucky Development Finance Authority, the Pennsylvania Industrial Development Authority, and the New York Development Authority (Sharp 1983). These authorities encourage development by making mortgage insurance and loans available to private firms, in order to assist them in purchasing land, buildings, and capital equipment (Sharp 1983, 30).

Perhaps the best known of these state-level development authorities is the New York Job Development Authority. State seed money helped to launch this public-purpose corporation in the 1960s. It is now funded through the sale of state-backed bonds to institutions and individuals and has become completely self-supporting. A nine-member board directs the Job Development Authority. The board consists of the state industrial commissioner, the state commissioner of commerce, and the state superintendent of banking (all ex officio members), and six members appointed by the governor with the approval of the state senate (Sharp 1983, 30).

Japan's Housing and Urban Development Corporation is a similar entity, operating at the national level. It reissues funds from housing bonds and loans (government loans, private loans, and initial capital from national and municipal governments). Its chief functions are to supply housing and encourage urban redevelopment (Housing and Urban Development Corporation 1989).

The closest counterpart to Japan's HUDC in the United States was the New York State Urban Development Corporation (UDC) of the late 1960s and early 1970s. It was perhaps the most powerful state or federal agency ever created in the United States to develop housing and generate new towns. Its extensive powers included the capability to develop low- and moderate-income housing, induce economic development, provide public facilities, and override local building codes and zoning ordinances (Loewenstein 1978, 261). At the height of its influence, it had undertaken approximately $1.5 billion in projects, which included 117 housing developments and 3 new towns (Loewenstein 1978, 261). It was unable to achieve self-sufficiency, however, and collapsed in 1975. Despite a recovery effort, the agency never regained its position of power (Loewenstein 1978).

Nevertheless, the UDC remains an important state economic development agency in New York. It no longer builds housing or entire new towns, but it retains its powers to condemn land, purchase property at interest rates below the market rate, float bonds, and override local ordinances. Its duties focus largely on industrial and commercial development (New York State Urban Development Corporation 1988).

Local Economic Development Corporations

Sometimes called community development corporations or industrial development corporations, local economic development corporations (EDCs) are also semipublic local development authorities. The public sector creates and partially finances them (Gilmore 1960). They also raise money by selling stocks and bonds, issuing notes, or soliciting contributions (Gilmore 1960). They are semipublic because their purpose is to generate community economic development, not to realize a profit. Because they have a strong private affiliation, they are often more effective in dealing with prospective firms than is the local government. EDCs help manufacturing firms by rehabilitating abandoned factories or constructing new ones, then leasing this space to them. They also make loans to businesses for constructing new plants, purchasing land or equipment, paying relocation costs, and so on (Gilmore 1960). A primary activity of local EDCs in the United States has been the floating of private-purpose tax-exempt bonds (see "Tax-Exempt Revenue Bonds").

Downtown Development Authorities

A downtown development authority (DDA) is an organization created to help revitalize a declining downtown. DDAs are excellent examples of organizations devised to carry out public-private partnerships. State enabling laws and local ordinances often give powers that allow them to act as both small governments and private companies in appropriate situations. They look like little municipalities. They have jurisdictional boundaries and a governing board made up of owners of homes, businesses, or real property within that jurisdiction. In many states they have taxation power and can float tax-exempt municipal bonds. They also may serve as a tax increment finance authority (see "Tax Increment Financing"). One of their most common activities is to improve the public infrastructure in their jurisdiction (Lyons and Hamlin 1991).

They also have the power to invest in businesses, lend to firms, build and own real estate, and earn a surplus from successful business ventures. In this way they are more like EDCs.

Private Corporations with a Public Purpose

Nonprofit Corporations

In the United States a nonprofit corporation can be either a stockholder or a membership organization. It may be formed to carry out a limited set of activities that are deemed to be for the public good. Because of the public benefit from these activities, the corporation may be granted nonprofit status at each of three levels.

First, the state that charters it will designate it as nonprofit if its articles of incorporation and bylaws produce an appropriate organizational structure and scope of activity to meet state requirements. Second, the U.S. Internal Revenue Service may grant the corporation tax-exempt status if it meets their criteria. The most coveted IRS designation is 501(c)3. With this designation, any surplus revenues are tax exempt, and donations by private individuals to the corporation are often tax deductible (Lyons and Hamlin

1991). Third, the local government may independently determine its exemption from local property, income, and sales taxes.

Stockholders of nonprofits cannot make a profit from their stock, and nonprofits are, in general, restricted in competing with for-profits. Nonprofits can engage in a wide variety of business activities, such as making loans and investments, buying and rehabilitating real estate, and entering into partnerships with other individuals and businesses. Nonprofits also can form for-profit subsidiaries or enter into joint ventures that can engage in any legal business as long as the subsidiary pays taxes on its profits before distributing dividends to the founding nonprofit organization (Lyons and Hamlin 1991). Foundations, municipalities, and community development organizations are examples of nonprofit organizations that may engage in community economic development.

Since donations to tax-exempt organizations are often tax deductible, nonprofits can generate substantial corporate equity. They accept donations from wealthy for-profit corporations and individuals attempting to avoid income and inheritance taxes. This equity may then be used to leverage other private investments. Such organizations can, for example, form a joint venture with a for-profit organization such that cash surpluses are funneled to the nonprofit and all tax advantages are given to the taxpaying corporation, providing maximum benefit to both. The equity of the joint venture can then be used to attract limited partnership equity or debt capital. Once the project is under way, the nonprofit corporation can recycle its earnings into other activities (Lyons and Hamlin 1991).

Nonprofit corporations do not exist in every country. In some cases they exist to facilitate liability protection for board members and officers but do not have strong tax advantages. Based on court rulings in recent years, board members and officers of nonprofits receive little liability protection in most states of the United States.

For-Profit Corporations with a Public Purpose

Any corporation may be established to carry out a public purpose. Its articles of incorporation may require that the board of directors represent a cross section of the community, and may restrict the activities in which it may engage. The founders may have reasons why they do not want to pursue nonprofit status. A local certified development corporation is an example of such an organization in the United States. A certified development corporation may be organized as being for profit, but in order to receive U.S. Small Business Administration certification, its board of directors must broadly represent the diverse interests of the community, and it must refrain from certain for-profit activities. The primary purpose for its existence is to act as a conduit for federally guaranteed, second-position, small-business real estate loans (Lyons and Hamlin 1991). A Business and Industrial Development Corporation (see "BIDCO Financing") is also typically a for-profit corporation with a public purpose.

In Japan, Minato Mirai 21 is an example of a private, for-profit local development corporation organized specifically for one public benefit project. Some of its shareholders are in the public or quasipublic sector (see "Equity Capital" for a further discussion of its activities).

The best example of a private for-profit corporation with a public purpose is found at the national level in the United States. It is the Federal National Mortgage Association (FNMA, or Fannie Mae). Originally established as a federal government corporation, FNMA became a private corporation in 1968. With stock traded on the New York Stock Exchange, it has 30,000 stockholders (Flick 1987). Its connection to the government is maintained through the five members of its board of directors appointed by the president of the United States (Flick 1987). Fannie Mae operates under a mortgage-backed security program. It buys loans, repackages them into securities, and sells these to private investors (Flick 1987).

ACTIVITIES

A purpose in establishing collaborative arrangements for urban revitalization that cross sectoral boundaries is to influence development in a specified area. This purpose assumes that the community recognizes that problems or opportunities exist in the designated area (Fosler and Berger 1982). The benefits brought to such a partnership by the public sector include the legal, political, and large-scale service provision advantages not available to the private sector working alone. The private sector brings the investment in labor, capital, and know-how sought by the government. In this relationship each entity carries out the tasks for which it was created in harmonious concert for mutual and, it is hoped, communitywide, benefit. In this respect, cross-sectoral alliances represent democratic and capitalistic principles in their purest form (Lyons and Hamlin 1991).

Key to the establishment of these partnerships is local initiative, which includes strong civic foundations and capable leadership (Fosler and Berger 1982). The elements of a strong civic foundation include communitywide concern; openness to public participation in the decision-making process; community vision; awareness of local strengths and weaknesses; effective civic groups; networking among community leaders; a nurturing environment for civic entrepreneurs; and continuity and flexibility in policy (Fosler and Berger 1982; Sorkin, Ferris, and Hudak 1986). A civic foundation with these characteristics will tend to spawn the kind of leadership necessary to create public-private partnerships for urban revitalization.

The leader(s) may come from either sector, and rarely come from both. In most cases, one sector takes the lead and the other assumes the role of facilitator (Fosler and Berger 1982). The same rules apply when third-sector entities are among the partners. Once the partnership is in place, leaders must focus upon the activities that will enable it to achieve its established goals.

The following section is a more detailed discussion of these public development-inducing activities. Its organization follows a standard outline of the needs of a business firm. This format was chosen because it is private firms' behavior that the public sector is attempting to influence. The relevant categories are land and related capital, labor, energy, finance, management, taxes, and research. Within this outline, subcategories of activities are described. The final subsection talks about focusing and integrating all other activities in a single project area. Table 3 lists partnership activities and indicates some relationships between them.

Land and Related Capital

Land Location, Acquisition, and Assembly Assistance

As discussed in Chapter 3, the marketplace for urban land suffers from several imperfections. In older areas experiencing urban decline, externalities related to land are particularly problematic. The public sector in most countries can use its special powers to assist private developers in overcoming some of the problems related to their need for land, in order to promote economic development and urban redevelopment.

In its simplest form, one approach is to help locate suitable parcels for the type of development being sought by a business. This serves to reduce the time and effort a private developer must put into site location research. Aided by the increased use of geographic information system (GIS) technologies (see Chapter 9), many cities maintain a computerized inventory of available vacant land within their jurisdictions. This provides site-specific information on zoning, acreage, street location, assessed value, and terrain and other development constraints (Carlson and Duffy 1985). This type of assistance makes the urban area that offers it considerably more attractive

Table 3
Activities of Intersectoral Partnerships

Land/Related Capital	Energy	Management
Land Acquisition	Conservation	Feas. Studies
Land Assembly	-rationing	
Phys. Improvements	-weatherization	
Excess Condemnation	-cogeneration	**Tax Incentives**
Land Readjustment	-incentives	
Land Write-Downs	Renewable Resources	Exemptions
Zoning Incentives		Abatements
Air Rights/TDR	**Finance**	Enterprise Zones
		TIF
Labor	Debt Capital	
	-direct loans	**Markets**
Labor Force Training	-debentures	
-recruiting/screening	-subord. debentures	Stabilization
-industrial training	-depository selectivity	Export Progs.
-retraining	-tax-exempt bonds	Procurement
	-second position on loan	
	-buy loans in sec. market	**Research**
	-loan guarantees	
	-LIF/risk pooling	Consultation
	Direct Equity Injections	Univ. R&D
	-common stock	
	-preferred stock	
	-convertible bonds	
	-royalty agreements	
	-warrants	
	-limited partnership units	
	-limited part. prefer. units	
	Indirect Equity Injections	
	Direct Subsidies	

to private investors because of reduced opportunity cost. This service is both for outsiders looking to come into a region and for existing business looking to expand.

Local governments may seek to assist private developers in acquiring land so as to reduce the cost of development. A private developer typically must assemble several parcels of urban land to have enough space for a modern development. In older areas of a city, chaotic subdivision of land, characterized by irrational lot lines that result in odd-shaped or small plots, impedes parcel assemblage for development. Because some landowners may resist selling until they can get a higher price because their parcel is essential for a new development project, the process of assembling land may become cumbersome, slow, and exorbitantly expensive. Government can help by using its power of eminent domain to buy and assemble parcels for a large development project and then sell them to a private developer. One can argue that this intervention by government into the real estate market does not distort the market but, rather, perfects it by making real estate more liquid and more functional (Lyons and Hamlin 1991).

Land Banking

In some countries, land in deteriorating areas becomes very inexpensive due to urban decline and the problems with irregular parcels. Some land-owners in arrears on taxes may abandon their property rather than pay. In other cases, government may acquire property in order to tear down vacant buildings blighting the community. Rather than reselling this property at the depressed price, many cities retain ownership, creating a "land bank." Such land is accumulated until parcels are large enough to facilitate significant modern development. It is not necessarily vacant land. Usable structures can be leased during the accumulation period (Blakely 1994). In Hungary, where local government owns a high percentage of commercial and industrial land as a result of the 1991 transition from Communist rule, officials would be wise to hold on to property in older areas rather than privatize it, so as to have the flexibility to readapt that property to modern use when the need arises.

Land Improvements

Physical improvements to the land refer to the improvements in a city's infrastructure (NASDA, CUED, and the Urban Institute 1983). Infrastructure, broadly defined, is "the set of those life-support and public facility systems which must be provided in order to enable the development of healthy human settlements" (Dajani 1978). Infrastructure systems in urban areas include roads, public transit, schools, water treatment facilities, street lighting, power transmission lines, sewer facilities, and parks and other recreational facilities (Levy 1988; Juergensmeyer 1985; Dajani 1978).

While most infrastructure is clearly in the public domain, its quality is crucial to the success of private development, thus creating an important point of intersectoral collaboration. Government can have a significant effect on development by consciously concentrating its limited infrastructure resources in high-priority locations, such as new industrial parks or redevelopment areas (Lyons and Hamlin 1991).

Excess Condemnation

Excess condemnation is taking, by right of eminent domain, more property than is necessary for the creation of a public improvement and, after completing the project, selling or leasing this excess. On the theory that the value of the excess lands will have increased by virtue of their proximity to the improvement, it is held to be within the power of government to sell these lands at a higher price to an appropriate user. In other words, the local government makes a profit on the sale of land surrounding the public improvement and uses this profit to help pay for the improvement (Lyons and Hamlin 1991).

Some argue that this practice puts government in the real estate speculation business. Others argue that the government project caused the surrounding land to increase in value, not action taken by private owners. If government does not use excess condemnation, then private landowners experience speculative gains in wealth without having added any value to society to justify those gains. Furthermore, a major public project may induce rapid development of surrounding land that may not be its long-term highest and best use. The resulting development pattern may, in fact, diminish the usefulness of the original public improvement. The clogging of expressway interchanges is an example (Lyons and Hamlin 1991). For these reasons, U.S. courts have upheld excess condemnation as a legitimate exercise of government powers (Steiss 1975). The Hungarian constitution also affords this right, although few local officials are well schooled in its use.

An example of effective use of excess condemnation occurs when a local government, planning to build a new airport, condemns more land than is necessary to accommodate the airport. Then, after leaving enough room for airport expansion, it develops an industrial park surrounding the airport, selling the prime industrial land for more than the original condemnation price (Lyons and Hamlin 1991).

The Japanese government implements a form of excess condemnation through its land readjustment law (described in the following section). Each pre-project property owner contributes land to HUDC as a part of the real estate trade process. This contribution represents a kind of condemnation. Often the aggregate amount of land contributed to HUDC is more than is necessary for infrastructure. The excess condemnation or "reserve land" then belongs to HUDC, usually as one parcel, and becomes a profit or surplus generator for HUDC (Minerbi et al. 1986). HUDC can then sell it, lease it, or develop it for financial gain. Since HUDC is a nonprofit corporation, theoretically the surplus is used to offset the cost of building the infrastructure and/or to reduce the cost of housing units built on the project (Hamlin and Lyons 1989).

Land Readjustment

Through negotiation between property owners, land readjustment re-draws property lines in a given redevelopment area so as to produce more rational and functional parcels of land, and allow for the modernization of infrastructure. This is done with a minimum number of property transac-tions or the use of condemnation. To the extent possible, land remains in the hands of the original owners in approximately the same proportion and location as before the readjustment (Lyons and Hamlin 1991).

Government has an important role in this process as intermediary agent between property owners. Presumably, in the right urban circumstances, property owners would be anxious to engage in this process because resulting parcels would be more valuable on the real estate market and more usable for modern development. Government would most likely be one of the property owners, as the owner of rights-of-way and public facilities (Lyons and Hamlin 1991).

Land readjustment is most effective where (1) location affords high development potential but (2) antiquated parcel sizes and shapes and anti-quated rights-of-way retard that development potential, and (3) existing above-ground improvements have low value relative to the potential value of the land. In short, land readjustment is useful where historic ownership patterns are keeping land from being put to its highest and best use. A prime candidate for this activity could be an antiquated and deteriorated district on the fringe of a prosperous central business district (CBD). It might also prove valuable in the development of an industrial park in an urban fringe area that previously had poor subdivision control (Lyons and Hamlin 1991).

Japan has used land readjustment extensively. Cultural factors and high land values make land readjustment an important alternative redevelopment method, and the Japanese Land Readjustment Law is one of the major tools of public-private partnership and urban renewal in that country. The cultural importance of family landownership makes the purchase or condemnation of land difficult there (Lyons and Hamlin 1991).

The Japanese development profession has used land readjustment for a wide array of development endeavors, including inner city redevelopment, fringe development, and new towns. The Land Readjustment Law is more complex than the simple description provided above. Under the system, a development agency (often HUDC) defines a project area. It then works with the property owners inside the project area to create a development plan. Property owners may be home owners, store owners, industrial corporations, railroads, governmental agencies, or any other legal entity.

As part of the implementation of the plan, property lines are redrawn to create parcels that are more conducive to real estate development and to the construction of modern infrastructure. Small parcel owners, such as house owners, may need to be compensated for their parcel with cash or with ownership in the final development project, such as a condominium unit. In all cases owners are given an option that constitutes a real estate trade so as to avoid a legal sale, which would require the payment of capital gains taxes. Because of rapidly rising land values in the postwar era, capital gains taxes can be a severe penalty for participation in a redevelopment project, and fear of such taxation has retarded or constrained redevelopment. As a result, the "trade" provision is an important inducement to cooperation with a land readjustment project (Hamlin and Lyons 1989).

Once property lines are readjusted, HUDC begins physical implementation of the project plan through the construction of modern infrastructure. An example is widened and realigned roads. The HUDC might also construct multiple-use utility tunnels for telephone, electrical, and water lines (Hamlin and Lyons 1989).

After infrastructure modernization, landowners may develop their land in general accordance with the project plan that has been agreed upon and sanctioned by law. Public landowners may develop parks, community centers, or other public facilities that enhance the overall development and further induce the private owners to build according to the plan. Private developers may sell or lease their land to HUDC, which then earns a surplus by developing the site. They can also hire HUDC to build and manage a project owned by the landowner (Hamlin and Lyons 1989).

A common feature of land readjustment is that each current landowner is typically offered a slightly smaller parcel after readjustment than she or he initially held. This contribution by each landowner, often as much as 35 percent, is primarily to provide the additional space needed by modern infrastructure, such as wider streets. Despite the reduction in ownership area, his or her holding should be significantly higher in value than before readjustment. A more rational shape to the parcel and the improved infrastructure greatly increase its development potential.

Often the aggregate amount of land contributed is more than is necessary for infrastructure. The excess is consolidated, through the redrafting of boundaries, into one large parcel. A quasigovernmental corporation, such as the Housing and Urban Development Corporation of Japan (HUDC), a New York Urban Development Corporation-type organization, takes ownership of the resultant parcel. This contribution is payment to HUDC for its coordination function and for its investment in infrastructure. The parcel becomes a "profit" sector that HUDC can sell, lease, or develop to generate revenues to pay for its contribution to the project. This process functions as a kind of voluntary excess condemnation.

The book *Land Readjustment: The Japanese System* provides a thorough examination of the land readjustment policy in Japan (Minerbi et al. 1986). The study's purpose was to offer policy makers in Hawaii a basis with which to judge the appropriateness of this development tool for their situation. Hawaii faces development problems similar to those of Japan, given the islands' location and limited development area (Lyons and Hamlin 1991).

Germany, Australia, South Korea, and Taiwan also use this technique (Schnidman 1988). Most of these countries have engaged in land readjustment projects for many years (Schnidman 1988). Recently, communities in the United States have tried activities similar to land readjustment that carry such names as commercial development pooling, negotiated replatting, and residential neighborhood polling (Schnidman 1988). Oregon, for example, uses negotiated replatting to modernize "antiquated subdivisions" in rural areas (Nelson and Recht 1988). Land readjustment was first used in the United States in 1791, when George Washington employed it to implement Pierre L'Enfant's plan for Washington, D.C. (Schnidman 1988). While current U.S. approaches to land readjustment are "watered down" relative to the system in other countries, they provide examples of the melding of land assembly and public-private partnership activities to achieve local economic development.

James L. Northrup (1986) tells the story of Dallas's use of what he calls an "assemblage partnership" to revitalize its Farmers Market district. It is home to a large municipal produce market covering approximately 100 acres.

Landowners in the district, including the Southern Pacific Railroad, the city, and a number of warehousing operations, were concerned about declining land values and the general deterioration of this fringe area of the downtown. The private landowners in this group formed a partnership that served as the single owner of their combined properties. Additional investors were attracted to purchase other privately held parcels. All told, the private partnership gained control of over forty-five acres in the district, and the city controlled forty-seven acres of its own. Recognizing the mutual benefit to be gained from working together, the private partnership and the city entered into a partnership for the redevelopment of the area by negotiating property exchanges and cost-sharing agreements for needed public improvements (Lyons and Hamlin 1991).

The partnership then negotiated with James Rouse's Enterprise Development Company to build a festival marketplace in the district to act as an anchor for leveraging further development. The private partners realized substantial profits by selling off their assembled parcel to a development syndicate that carried the project forward with the Enterprise Development Company. The city gained both an attractive, well-planned, and economically viable addition to its central business district and the resultant property tax revenues (Lyons and Hamlin 1991).

While U.S. examples represent a weaker version of land readjustment than is found in other countries, the potential for applying the model to the U.S. situation in the foreseeable future is strong. States such as California, Hawaii, and Florida have studied the adoption of land readjustment enabling legislation (Schnidman 1988).

Land Write-Downs

A land write-down occurs when a government or quasigovernmental agency sells land to a private business for less than the market price. The public sector may originally have acquired the land through eminent domain as a part of a land assembly program, may have confiscated it for taxes in arrears, or may have held it in the city's land bank. City governments frequently use this inducement to encourage development of parcels in the central city that might otherwise remain vacant or underdeveloped. Significant infrastructure improvements and boundary readjustments often are made before sale. Sometimes the land is sold for $1.00 or given away if the developer agrees to develop it in accordance with the city's plan. Land write-downs are used in many countries.

Land Use Control Incentives

While zoning regulations and other land use controls have been viewed by many in recent years as barriers to development, this planning tool was created in the late nineteenth and early twentieth centuries as a means of protecting property values and encouraging investment. After the phenomenal growth of urban areas in the 1950s and 1960s, zoning was used by many local governments in the United States to slow and redirect growth, thus making it appear to be anti-growth (Lyons and Hamlin 1991). Today, localities employ land use controls as an incentive to private investment. Some examples are described below.

Incentive zoning has been a popular approach to encouraging development in America's large cities, at the same time promoting open space, landscaping, public art, and other cultural amenities. Most incentive zoning permits developers to build higher (more floors than the base zoning ordinance allows) in exchange for the provision of a public plaza, or other amenities, on the site. An example of successful incentive zoning is Chicago's First National Plaza. The developer built a large terraced plaza, with an attractive display of public art and a staging area for outdoor entertainment in the summer, in exchange for the right to add several stories to the First National Bank Tower on the same site. Developers have responded well to the opportunity to build at higher densities. In New York City, incentive zoning has been so successful in developing portions of Manhattan that the city has had to eliminate it in those areas to prevent overbuilding (Lyons and Hamlin 1991).

Performance zoning also can be used as an inducement to development. It allows uses that may be considered incompatible to be located adjacent to each other, provided they are carefully sited and properly screened. The standards that must be met by these adjacent land uses are quantified, and therefore less subjective than those of traditional zoning ordinances. Private developers find that their costs often are reduced by performance zoning because of its greater flexibility with regard to land use and the benefits derived from the clustering of development, which this technique encourages.

Mixed use developments (MXDs) allow multiple uses on a single site, usually including retail, office, residential, and recreational uses. The separation of land uses through land use controls has been more strictly applied in the United States than in most other countries, sometimes to the detriment of innovative development. Developers like the additional markets that mixed use developments open to them and the reduction in risk that a multiple use development affords. Among other advantages, built-in markets for retail activities are created. MXDs make sense from a planning perspective as well, in that they encourage internal and pedestrian traffic in the central city, as opposed to automobile traffic coming in from the outside (Lyons and Hamlin 1991).

Air Rights and Transfer of Development Rights

Many cities have adopted a policy of selling air rights to private developers in order to induce central city investment. The concept of air rights dates back to common law, wherein fee simple ownership of land included not only the real property at ground level but also the space extending below the parcel to the center of the earth and above it to the sky (Donohoe 1988).

Much of the land located in central cities is owned by the government, including public buildings, parking structures, highways, parks, and sports facilities. Most of these public facilities do not make full use of their air rights, nor is it likely they will do so in the future. Some enterprising cities are selling these air rights to private developers, who are permitted to use them to increase the intensity of development in targeted renewal areas.

Private development might be built over a public facility. An example would be an office complex built above a public parking lot or a submerged urban expressway. In other cases the rights are transferred to another parcel, in a transfer of development rights. The parcel of land receiving the additional development rights may be adjacent to, or on the same block as, the land from which the rights are being sold. In other cases, development rights may be transferred greater distances (Schlefer 1984). The city generates revenue from this sale for reinvestment in public infrastructure or the provision of other public services, and the developer obtains the right to build at greater densities than local ordinances might otherwise permit (Lyons and Hamlin 1991).

Labor

Structural Unemployment

As mechanization continues to replace manual labor in nearly every part of the world, the skills, talents, and attitudes of the local labor force become more critical. An important alliance between the public goals of the community and private success focuses on education and training of the workforce.

Time and talent are perishable resources, so not utilizing the labor force to its fullest is a terrible loss to the individual, the community, and the economy. Structural unemployment and underemployment refer to the subset of individuals who are not employed or are not fully utilizing their abilities because of a mismatch between the skills in demand in a given location and the skills available. Because of the locational facet of structural employment, communities and individuals can be big winners if they partner with business to reduce structural unemployment.

Labor Force Training

Local governments in the United States and elsewhere have become involved in training and retraining local workforces. This is not surprising, given the dramatic economic restructuring that has gone on. With the decline in traditional heavy industry and the rise of high-technology businesses, an appropriately skilled labor pool is a very valuable resource for a city seeking to attract development. A study reported in *Area Development* magazine found that "availability of skilled labor" was third on the list of the top twenty site selection factors from 1989 to 1993, and was increasing in importance (Laughlin and Taft 1995). If a locality can successfully anticipate the demand for skilled labor by the private sector and meet that demand, it can gain an advantage in the market for new development (Lyons 1987). Several methods the public sector uses to provide skilled labor as an inducement to private urban development are described below.

Recruiting and Screening. Nearly all state governments in the United States provide the service of recruiting and screening employees for firms operating in their state. The state's employment security division, or its counterpart, normally offers this service. The local offices in cities through-out the state maintain regularly updated, computerized data banks on job opportunities and labor availability. Participating firms receive a list of qualified applicants for each advertised job opening, based on this data and an interview process. This service saves firms time and money (Lyons and Hamlin 1991).

Industrial Training. Industrial training programs are a more proactive nonfinancial incentive often provided by the public sector. The majority of these are customized to prepare workers for employment in specific indus-tries, or individual businesses, that are the focus of public-sector planning efforts (NASDA, CUED, and the Urban Institute 1983). Government can, in this way, select the firms it wishes to encourage to invest in the local community by offering specialized training. Public universities or commu-nity colleges in the area often develop these programs, and sometimes offer them at the business site or through distance-learning technology. The cost of the program is typically shared by some combination of the business, the state and local governments, the institution of higher education involved, and perhaps labor unions.

Retraining. Government retraining programs seek to lure investment by certain firms by providing a more appropriately skilled workforce. This service has been very important in recent years in the heavy manufacturing states of the northeastern and midwestern United States. These areas have experienced numerous manufacturing plant closings and "downsizing" activities, leaving thousands of persons without jobs and without the necessary skills to obtain new ones. By retraining these individuals, the public sector helps to reduce unemployment while establishing an attractive labor pool (Lyons and Hamlin 1991).

Employability Training. Training must be perceived broadly. Despite current trends toward training as a solution to structural unemployment, job-specific training, although important, is best described as the necessary icing on the cake. Occupational training cannot be utilized by the individual until other kinds of skills are acquired. To take advantage of training programs, an individual must have sufficient language and computational skills. A large percentage of individuals with labor market problems do not have satisfactory competence in basic skills. Also, an individual must be prepared to cope psychologically and socially with the labor market. No level of training or other assistance will enable an individual to obtain and maintain work if this prerequisite is not met. The coping concept refers to several personal attributes. Central to coping is a positive self-concept. A person who has a positive self-image is in a better position to relate well to fellow employees and supervisors, be self-motivated, and have a positive attitude about work. Self-concept development also creates assertiveness in less assertive individuals and enables one to be realistic about one's career aspirations. A sound self-concept is imperative for an individual to deal emotionally with periods of cyclical unemployment and to avoid problems of health and home relations that may transform cyclical economic problems into chronic physical, economic, and social disorders (Muth, Hamlin, and Stuhmer 1979).

Energy

One need only consider the effects of the oil shocks of the 1970s on the world economy to appreciate the importance of readily available and relatively inexpensive energy to successful local economic development. When a major source of energy becomes scarce and expensive, industries that rely on it are adversely affected. Firms may find they must reduce their production or relocate if adequate supplies of reasonably priced energy are not available at their current locations.

Two important considerations that must be addressed by local economic development planners are (1) the supply of relevant types of energy for local users and (2) the cost of this energy. As the Rocky Mountain Institute points out, eighty to ninety cents of every dollar spent for energy is permanently lost to the local community (Browning and Lovins 1989).

Ensuring sufficient affordable energy entails several activities: conservation of existing nonrenewable sources, effective use of renewable sources, and development of totally new alternatives. Because the energy industry is replete with public and private organizational types, an understanding of intersectoral partnerships is crucial to all of these activities. Nonrenewable sources of energy are oil, natural gas, and other fossil fuels. Solar, wind, and water power are examples of renewable energy sources (Lyons and Hamlin 1991).

Numerous techniques have been used for conserving nonrenewable sources. The most dramatic of these is rationing, in which each user is given a fixed allotment over a specific time period. This technique is normally reserved for emergency situations, because it greatly limits economic activity. At the other end of the spectrum is self-policing, leaving responsibility with the individual user to employ only as much energy as is essential to its operations. Between these extremes lie a number of methods for conserving nonrenewable energy sources, or encouraging their conservation, that are useful to local community economic development planning (Lyons and Hamlin 1991).

Weatherizing buildings in cold climates is one approach to conservation. Local governments can partner with local utilities to save energy dollars by underwriting the cost of aerial and ground-level infrared analysis. Heat-sensitive film picks up points of heat loss in buildings. When these photographs are shown to local firms and homeowners, they are able to target portions of their buildings that are in need of weatherization. This is a relatively inexpensive way to foster good public-private relations and conserve fossil fuels (Lyons and Hamlin 1991). Distribution of information instructing residents and businesses on conservation techniques may also have a big payoff.

Some publicly and privately owned utilities have established cogeneration plants, which reuse waste heat. This not only saves renewable energy sources but also may attract business because it constitutes a new energy resource (Browning and Lovins 1989). Wisconsin Power and Light Company offers five-year contracts for shared-savings energy efficiency projects to firms in its service area. These projects include cogeneration activities and energy retrofitting. They are commonly established as joint ventures involving the firm, a local bank, and Wisconsin Power and Light (Browning and Lovins 1989). Under a shared savings arrangement, both the utility and the user benefit from the savings realized through increased efficiency (Browning and Lovins 1989). This usually more than offsets the cost of the equipment installed to achieve the savings (Lyons and Hamlin 1991).

Offering financial incentives to firms that adopt conservation strategies is another approach to energy conservation. Legislation at the state level is helpful in this endeavor. Minnesota established an Energy Development Loan Program and an Energy Loan Insurance Program, which provide direct loans and loan guarantees, respectively, to firms to encourage energy conservation (NASDA 1986). Alaska offers a credit on its corporate income tax of up to 35 percent of the cost of installing an energy conservation system (NASDA 1986). A 25 percent tax credit for the installation of energy conservation devices that cost more than $6,000 is offered to businesses in

California (NASDA 1986). Local economic development planners can encourage and instruct firms in the use of tax incentives.

Greater use of solar, wind, geothermal, and hydroelectric energy can both increase and diversify the local energy supply. For example, numerous local governments have adopted ordinances that permit, with some restrictions, wind energy conversion devices (windmills) within city limits. Wind farms—fields full of windmills whose power is harnessed to generate electricity—are now found throughout the world (Browning and Lovins 1989). At present, commercial "wind farms" can be found in California, Hawaii, Massachusetts, Montana, New Hampshire, New York, Oregon, Vermont, and Wyoming (Browning and Lovins 1989).

Local entrepreneurs in Colton, California, parlayed the use of solar energy into profits for themselves and jobs for the local community by using a federal grant to hire local young people to construct and install solar devices. In essence, a new industry that became a boon to the local economy and fostered the use of a renewable energy resource was created (Browning and Lovins 1989).

Small dams may be a source of energy and income for a community. Approximately 50,000 small dams (defined as less than 100 feet in height) exist in the United States. Many of these currently produce some energy, and another large portion did generate power but were abandoned in the 1960s, when energy seemed cheap. The current level of energy costs, however, has again made electricity production feasible at such dams. This feasibility, combined with the emergence of new technologies, such as the bulb turbine, has increased the viability of small hydro as a salient energy source (Clark et al. 1979). Through a combination of public and private initiatives, these dams can be rehabilitated and retrofitted to produce a low-cost and reliable source of energy for the community's economic base. The retrofit process also produces jobs, and the area surrounding the dam can be an attractive and unusual green space and recreation area (Lyons and Hamlin 1991).

One example of a retrofitted dam is on the Huron River near Belleville, Michigan. The local government (Van Buren Township) worked with the Ayres, Lewis, Norris and May engineering firm and the Trade Union Leadership Council of Michigan to retrofit the small dam for hydroelectric generation while employing and training disadvantaged youth from Detroit to prepare them for entry into the building trades. Belleville Lake and the area surrounding the dam are also important community amenities (Lyons and Hamlin 1991).

State legislation pertaining to the use of renewable energy resources also is abundant. Colorado, for example, does not include the appreciation in value caused by the installation of a solar, wind, or geothermal energy system in determining the value of a building for tax purposes (NASDA 1986). Indiana reduces taxes on properties that employ hydroelectric power devices (NASDA 1986). Wood products to be used for heating are exempted from sales and use taxes in Maryland (NASDA 1986).

Efforts continue toward the development of new alternatives to existing energy resources. Gasohol for powering vehicles and equipment is one example. A number of local communities have put their public fleets on gasohol. Many state governments have offered financial incentives to businesses whose corporate fleets use gasohol (NASDA 1986). Governments, often through research universities, are investing large sums in research on new fuels (Lyons and Hamlin 1991).

The importance of energy to state and local economic development has become widely recognized. Local and state governments are partnering with the private sector to ensure that ample, affordable energy is available to keep local economies functioning (Lyons and Hamlin 1991).

Finance

As described in Chapter 2, financial intermediaries are at the center of the economic development process, acting as the bridge between the critical functions of savings and investment. An alliance between public purpose and private purpose has always been critical to the intermediary process, yet seldom do intermediaries exist in enough variety to serve diverse economic needs. The process breaks down particularly in underdeveloped regions or areas of decline, such as low-income urban neighborhoods.

Understanding how to skillfully lubricate the financial intermediary system can benefit the local community in two ways: (1) by attracting investment capital to the area and (2) by inducing developers, industrialists, and other businesspersons to put that capital to work in ways that promote public goals. On the saver side of the equation, the secret is the ratio of risk to reward. One must either reduce the risk of putting savings into the desired investment vehicle or increase the reward. On the side of the business borrower, the intention is to make investment capital easier to acquire by making it more readily available and by reducing its cost. Several types of incentives may be employed to accomplish these goals. Some examples are described below.

Loan Guarantees

Loan guarantees provide backing for loans made by private lending institutions. If the recipient of the loan defaults, the government steps in to cover part or all of the losses. With this protection, private lenders experience less risk, and thus are more likely to lend to small businesses, other higher-risk firms, or businesses in at-risk neighborhoods. Or they may lower their interest rates (NASDA, CUED, and the Urban Institute 1983).

The backing for the loan may be the "full faith and credit" of the government or some other dependable quasipublic asset. "Full faith and credit" commits future tax revenues of the government to covering bad loans. Other assets include revolving loan fund balances and other dependable revenue streams.

If carefully implemented so that no loans experience problems, this method costs the government nothing. However, since the purpose of a loan guarantee program is to increase capital flow to higher-risk situations, loan guarantees are likely to result in some losses to taxpayers. By involving the private sector, the cost should be far less than if government acted alone. In this case, loan guarantees represent a kind of indirect subsidy to both lenders and borrowers for the sake of promoting public policy. It is a partnership in which all parties share in the risks and rewards.

Since the issue is how best to balance risks and rewards for both lender and borrower so as to induce desired economic activity, deciding the amount of the guarantee and the amount of the down payment is important. Decreasing the percentage of the loan that is guaranteed puts more of the risk on the lending institution, and increasing the down payment causes the borrower to be at greater risk.

Where possible, employing loan guarantees to promote public policy is preferable to lending money directly, since this approach maximizes use of existing private financial intermediary institutions and minimizes the impact on the natural marketplace. A difficult challenge is designing rules that focus investment on accomplishing public goals while opening the process sufficiently to provide a fair opportunity for all potential borrowers and lenders.

Loan Insurance

Private insurance companies also back loans, providing the same kind of lender risk reduction as governmental guarantees. The insurance companies are selective in the loans they will guarantee, preferring very large loans, so as to reduce processing and oversight costs. They charge a premium to cover their risk and provide a return on investment. This premium greatly increases the cost of the loan to the borrower. One alternative is for local government to subsidize the loan insurance premium for business ventures that clearly benefit targeted disadvantaged areas or otherwise promote public policy. In this way the public interest is pursued at minimal cost, using private investment systems.

Loan Insurance Fund or Risk Pooling Program

A loan insurance fund (LIF) or risk pooling program is a reserve fund established to insure future losses from a portfolio of loans that banking institutions make under the LIF program. It might be described as a kind of self-insurance or revolving insurance fund using an escrow account. LIF assists banks that wish to be more aggressive than normal in taking risk. As a result, it provides access to debt capital for many companies that cannot qualify for conventional bank financing, thereby providing badly needed medium-risk financial capital. LIF is different from the traditional loan guarantee program, which guarantees a percentage of a loan on a loan-by-loan basis. Instead, LIF is used to back a portfolio of loans.

A reserve fund is accumulated from a one-time premium charge paid by each borrower for each loan made under the program. This premium is matched by a payment contributed by the participant bank. These payments may also be matched by a small governmental subsidy from a quasigovernmental institution in charge of the LIF program. The resulting reserve is deposited by the quasigovernmental institution in the participating bank's name. The special reserve is owned and controlled by the quasigovernmental institution, but each participating bank has its own separate earmarked reserve, within the fund, that is used only to cover losses on its loans (Lyons and Hamlin 1991).

The premium payment is one of the terms of the loan, which is a private transaction between the bank and the borrower. Generally, the premium is based on the level of perceived risk. The program sets minimum and maximum premium limits based on a percentage of the loan. These limits help to determine how much of the risk and reward is shared by lender, borrower, and the public. The premium includes other up-front expenses to be financed by the loan (Lyons and Hamlin 1991).

Due to the payments that need to be made into the reserve, a loan under this program is likely to be more expensive to the borrower than conventional bank loans. This is to be expected because of the higher risk, but the program induces banks to provide more private investment capital for this range of risk than would otherwise be available.

BIDCO Financing

A business and industrial development corporation (BIDCO) is another arrangement to plug the medium-risk gap. The level of risk/reward with which BIDCOs deal is slightly higher than that for LIF programs.

Commercial banks are the primary source of debt capital in most communities, and a loan insurance pool can extend somewhat the level of risk banks can take. However, because the primary source of bank funds is deposits from the public, banks must be highly regulated institutions that focus on the low-risk, low-return end of the business financing market (Williams 1986). The savings and loan debacle that climaxed early in the 1990s illustrates dramatically what happens when the risk/reward and regulatory environments become unbalanced at depository institutions.

BIDCOs have been created to be nonbank lending institutions designed to serve business financing needs with risk/reward levels beyond those served by commercial banks, even with loan insurance funds. The BIDCO's source of capital is private investor equity, or the purchase of stock. As a result, government can provide a more relaxed regulatory environment to BIDCOs than that faced by banks. In addition, the public sector often furnishes these companies with debt and matching equity funding at below market rates. With this combination of resources and regulatory flexibility, BIDCOs make loans to small businesses unable to obtain traditional bank financing. These loans are at higher rates than bank loans, and BIDCOs can demand inclusion of a equity kicker (see below) not allowed to banks. The state of California established BIDCO financing in 1977, and other states, including Michigan, adapted the California law to their situation.

Micro Loan Program

This unusual form of financial intermediary draws investment funds to small start-up businesses. This is a niche that few other sources will touch because of the high risk and high service cost. Yet financing this sector is important to diversify the local economy and provide opportunities for individuals with good ideas but few traditional credentials or contacts to put their skills and imagination to work.

The program starts when a group of banks agree to make a loan to the micro loan pool. The program structure minimizes the risk to the bank. The funds are to be lent to a broad spectrum of businesses, and the program uses peer pressure strategies and risk pooling to insure repayment. These features will be described below. In the United States, banks often are willing to be involved because of the community service requirements of the Community

Reinvestment Act (CRA). The amount of the initial pool may be augmented with a donation from a local benefactor or a foundation, thereby decreasing the banks' risk still further. The local governmental body or a revolving loan fund of one of the quasigovernmental organizations also may participate in the initial loan to the pool.

The second step is for a program administrator to invite a limited number of micro businesses to participate. A micro business typically has three or fewer employees. Peer groups of approximately five businesses are formed. The peer group simultaneously serves as a social support group, a peer pressure group, and a financial risk cushion.

In the beginning each participant is allowed to take out a very small loan, perhaps $1,000, from the micro loan pool established by the initial bank loan. Often all members of the peer group must cosign each loan. The peer group meets regularly to assess progress and offer mutual personal and business support. Under the rules of some micro loan programs, if one member of the group cannot make the weekly payment, it must be paid by the others. When one participant successfully pays off a loan on schedule, he or she may graduate to a higher line of credit. Ultimately, as businesses grow, the peer group breaks up and participants begin dealing directly with the bank or other more traditional sources of credit.

Micro loan programs have become popular in such diverse places as Bangladesh and the Bronx. In Indonesia, the national family planning agency used World Bank Funds to establish village micro loan programs for women's groups. The purpose was not only to promote small business but also to teach business skills to women, giving them greater self-esteem and independence (Nystuen et al. 1991). In Louisville, Kentucky, the micro loan program was used to promote small business development in an inner city neighborhood as a part of the HANDS project, which is described in Chapter 5. Money to establish the original pool came from low-interest loans from three banks and a local foundation. In Hungary, a micro loan program helps that nation make the transition from command economy to free market. Local micro loan programs there receive half of their initial funding from the European Community and half from the Hungarian national government (To'th 1995).

Revenue Bonds

Another way for the public sector to attract and channel investment capital is to use its governmental powers to act as an intermediary. Often a governmental authority can promote the securitization of projects by acting as the issuer of revenue bonds and then lending money to the project from the proceeds. Typically this is done through a quasigovernmental corporation such as an economic development corporation or an industrial development authority, and the bond is called a private purpose revenue bond. In such cases, the government experiences no direct legal risk because the bond buyers rely upon the success of the project for repayment of the bond. The project's failure causing a default on the bond does not endanger the general fund of the community. Unfortunately, since the revenue bond is sold by the municipality, its financial reputation may be harmed in case of default.

Usually, enabling law requires demonstration of a public purpose before government may exercise this intermediary function. An example would be a redevelopment project in a declining area. The interest on these bonds may be either taxable or tax-exempt.

Tax-Exempt Revenue Bonds

Tax-exempt bonds, as the name implies, can be sold by the local government at a lower rate of interest because interest accrued is exempt from federal tax in the United States and from income tax in the state where they are issued. This amounts to an indirect interest subsidy, or low-interest loan, from the exempting government, via the intermediary local government, to the bond seller (NASDA, CUED, and the Urban Institute 1983). This mechanism does not seem to exist in Japan or Hungary, and varies from country to country. The method is not as effective in countries where income taxes are less important or where the effectiveness of tax collection is poor.

Tax-exempt revenue bonds must be sold through a public body, such as a municipality or a state government, in order to maintain their tax-exempt status. Usually the proceeds must be used for a public purpose, but often this public purpose can promote private real estate development. An example is the use of special assessment revenue bonds to build infrastructure needed by a project. In this way, the developer pays the city for needed infrastructure but uses tax-exempt financing through the special assessment process. Another example is municipal revenue bond financing that is used to building a parking structure important for a major private development project. Use of the structure must generate revenues to pay off the bonds, either through charging of user fees or by renting part or all of the structure to the adjacent development project (Lyons and Hamlin 1991).

A variety of private purpose tax-exempt bonds exist in the United States, the most common of which is the industrial revenue bond (IRB). In the early 1980s, prior to 1987 changes in U.S. income tax laws, IRBs were the most popular type of financial incentive for economic development (NASDA,

CUED, and the Urban Institute 1983). The projects allowed under IRB programs have included industrial buildings, warehouses, industrial parks, medical facilities, certain recreation facilities, and pollution control systems (*Site Selection Handbook* 1985). The tax reforms mentioned above, which went into effect in 1987, have eliminated commercial IRBs and approximately half of all tax-exempt revenue bond issues for industrial purposes (Lyons and Hamlin 1991).

Revenue Bond Insurance

Since revenue bonds are paid off through the success of a particular project, they are sometimes perceived as risky and illiquid, thereby forcing the interest rate up. For large projects, bond insurance is sometimes purchased from a company specializing in this activity. If the entire value of the bond is insured in this way, the rating of the bond may be that of the insuring company. The insurance premium is generally high, forcing up the cost of the loan to the borrower. The public sector may subsidize this insurance for projects it deems particularly important or may insure the bond itself, using quasipublic funds such as the balance on a revolving loan fund (see below). Saline, Michigan, for example, used the revenue stream from a tax increment financing district (described later) that included a new industrial park, to insure revenue bonds used to develop the industrial park and sell parcels to private firms.

Revolving Loan Funds

Local governments or their financial authorities sometimes make loans directly to private investors. In this way, the government assumes the role normally fulfilled by a commercial lending institution such as a bank. However, this should be a last resort, and government should become involved only if private lenders will not. Governments usually avoid competing directly with banks (Lyons and Hamlin 1991).

Interest rates on these loans may or may not be below market rate. In many cases these loans may be payable over a longer term than loans available from private lenders. Their greatest advantage is their availability to firms or investors that, due to their small size or the speculative nature of their operations, are unable to obtain capital from private lending institutions (NASDA, CUED, and the Urban Institute 1983).

The public sector typically places certain conditions upon direct loans to in order to ensure that the investment they induce is focused on the public interest. Revolving loan funds represent one means for administering direct loan programs (NASDA, CUED, and the Urban Institute 1983). Public and private monies are often used to establish revolving loan funds. When a loan is made from such a fund, the borrower repays the principal into the fund so that it is regularly replenished. Interest on the loan and processing fees are frequently used to cover the costs of administering the fund (Lyons and Hamlin 1991).

Loan funds with local governmental involvement exist throughout the world and are becoming more common as governments decentralize. In Hungary, municipal governments are given constitutional authority to make direct loans to businesses and/or establish revolving loan funds. The city of Szolnok, for example, is providing loans to developers (Hegedus 1995). In Japan, part of the proceeds from the privatization stock sale of NTT Corporation was put into revolving funds to loan to private business projects. In Korea, decentralization of governmental responsibilities to localities is a major national policy goal. Municipal policy makers, recently elected for the first time, are very interested in starting revolving loan funds and using other local development tools.

Subordinated Debentures

Generally a debenture is a certificate signed by an officer of a corporation as evidence of a debt. It is a bond backed by the general credit of a corporation rather than a particular asset. Debentures are purchased by investors or banks. A government or governmental authority can lend money to a local corporation by buying debentures from it.

A subordinated debenture is a debt instrument that is subordinated to other specified indebtedness of the borrowing company. In the event of dissolution, subordinated debt comes after other debt instruments when receiving payouts. As such it is more risky to the lender and to the investor buying the debenture, and may be difficult to sell to private investors. By purchasing debentures that are subordinated to a predetermined amount of bank loans, a governmental authority may be able to inject money into a company without diminishing the project's chances of receiving additional bank financing (Lyons and Hamlin 1991). This is because the bank's loan would have a superior position.

Depository Selectivity

Local governments occasionally have excess cash in their possession. They receive tax payments and other sources of revenues on an irregular basis, and must hold it until expenses are incurred or debt payments come due. Local governments, for example, tend to collect property taxes twice a year while making payment on expenditures all year long. One financial interface between the public sector and the private sector occurs when a government deposits cash reserves for temporary safekeeping. At any point in time, these reserves may be very large, dwarfing the amounts received from other depositors. They may, therefore, have a significant influence on the operation of the financial intermediary system (Lyons and Hamlin 1991).

Government deposits in banks are like very short-term loans to those institutions. Therefore, governments should make a conscious choice of where to put funds in the same way they would scrutinize the making of any direct loan. Safety of the deposit is a primary consideration. Return on investment is another, but the interest earned on very short-term investments will not vary widely from that on instruments of comparable risk (Lyons and Hamlin 1991).

One approach to cash management that a government may espouse is to temper its return on investment criterion for selecting money market vehicles with an understanding of the potential impact of these cash management decisions on other policy issues. One example of this would occur when a local government decides which bank will receive its cash deposit based in part on which bank is most cooperative in promoting local economic development. In other words, if the Fourth National Bank uses its deposits to make loans to the local community, while Bigger Bank and Trust deposits its funds in a larger money center bank, then the city government might be more inclined to deposit its excess short-term funds in Fourth National Bank. The cost to taxpayers of such a policy is the possible opportunity cost of earning a lower return on short-term investment. If the criteria for the choice of banks are open to the public and precisely delineated, the policy could be an effective means of leveraging more private debt capital for local business developers and home owners. The larger and longer the local government's deposits, the stronger the leverage power (Lyons and Hamlin 1991).

Second Position Loans

A second position loan is a loan in a subordinate position to another loan using the same real estate development as collateral. Assume, for example, that a mortgage loan is given to help finance a project worth $50 million and the loan is for 80 percent of the project cost. Then a second mortgage is given by a second source for the remaining 20 percent, or $10 million. In the case of default, the project would be sold and the proceeds would be used first to pay off the original mortgage. Remaining sale proceeds would then be used to pay off the second or subordinated position loan, to the extent possible. The second position loan clearly involves more risk, and therefore commands a higher rate of interest. If a government or quasigovernmental authority is willing to make a second position loan for 50 percent of the project cost, developers would have less difficulty finding private financing for the remaining 50 percent because the private financing would have senior position. In this way the public sector induces private financial institutions to become involved in projects in renewal areas that they otherwise might not enter (Lyons and Hamlin 1991).

Buying Loans in a Secondary Market

Buying loans in a secondary market is yet another way to reduce the cost and increase the supply of debt capital. In the primary market, commercial lending institutions make mortgage loans at market interest rates (Lyons and Hamlin 1991). In the secondary mortgage market, outstanding loans are traded when lenders need funds before their loans are completely amortized (Ammer and Ammer 1984). By selling these loans to other financial intermediaries in the secondary mortgage market, local banks free up funds to make new loans locally. To be marketable in the secondary market, mortgages typically must be written according to a standard "boiler plate." In this way they can be "bundled" with similar mortgages and sold in large denominations. Sometimes investors buy bonds on national bond market that are backed by the debt service from these bundles. In this chain of events, investors nationally buy bonds, thus allowing secondary mortgage institutions to buy bundles of mortgages, which allows local lenders to make more loans.

Three major secondary mortgage market institutions operate in the United States: the Federal National Mortgage Association (FNMA or Fannie Mae), the Government National Mortgage Association (GNMA or Ginnie Mae), and the Federal Home Loan Mortgage Corporation (FHLMC or Freddie Mac) (Flick 1987). FNMA is a private corporation with a public purpose, while GNMA and FHLMC are government corporations. Fannie Mae and Ginnie Mae purchase VA and FHA loans; Freddie Mac has developed a secondary market for loans without VA or FHA insurance (Flick 1987). The "Big Three," as they are sometimes called, continue to be an important source of mortgage money in the United States (Flick 1987). The secondary mortgage market should be distinguished from the primary market, where mortgages originate (Jones and Grebler 1961).

Equity Injections and Equity Kickers

Equity is a private firm's assets in excess of its liabilities. In the case of a corporation, the portion of equity that is owned by the holders of the firm's stock, both common and preferred, is known as corporate equity (Ammer and Ammer 1984). One way for the public to induce a firm to develop in a particular geographic area or in a particular way is for government to purchase ownership shares of the corporation. Government must be cautious about becoming involved in this type of transaction, however. It must prove that private corporate ownership is for the health, safety, and welfare of the general public, and that it does not adversely impact the rights of other shareholders of either this firm or competing firms. This type of incentive is typically used to induce developers to build in declining areas of the city where they would not otherwise become involved (Lyons and Hamlin 1991).

In the appropriate situation, injecting equity into a company or a project, through the purchase of stock or participation, can be a more effective mechanism for inducing development than providing debt capital. While facilitating loans to a project or a company can provide needed capital to promote development, it can also make the company's balance sheet less attractive by increasing its debt/equity ratio. This lessens its ability to receive additional financing from private sources. The injection of equity capital, on the other hand, improves the debt/equity ratio and increases the project's chances for private financing. In this way a small amount of government equity participation can leverage a large amount of private capital injection (Lyons and Hamlin 1991).

Viewing the situation in the opposite way, providing a comprehensive package of debt capital and cost reduction incentives to a firm can be expensive for the taxpayer. If the company succeeds, partially as a result of the incentive package, it may be appropriate for the public sector to participate financially in that success. The community will, of course, benefit from the jobs and tax base that result from the firm's success, but the government of the community may want to participate more directly through part ownership of the firm. It may require, in exchange for the incentive package, that the firm give it an "equity kicker" or part ownership in the business (Lyons and Hamlin 1991).

Equity financing can take several forms. Each type and how a government might participate directly are described below.

Common Stock. This form is a security that represents ownership of a share in a corporation. Common stockholders usually have a direct say in matters concerning corporate operations through a vote at the annual shareholders' meetings, but nonvoting shares are also possible. Owners of common stock bear more risk than either preferred stockholders or bondholders (see below) because they are the last to be paid should the corporation cease operations. On the other hand, they stand to realize greater payoffs in capital appreciation and dividends (Ammer and Ammer 1984). The government can encourage private investment by purchasing shares of common stock in private corporations whose activities it wants to influence or promote (Lyons and Hamlin 1991).

Local public ownership of businesses was historically rare but is becoming increasingly common. In Hungary, ownership of Communist-held businesses was turned over to local governments. Some municipalities are maintaining part or total ownership. Local development corporations in the United States are learning the process of negotiating equity kickers and stimulating venture capital, and as a result, end up in ownership positions.

Japanese governments seldom make direct purchases of common stock, but have been known to invest on a project basis in recent years. An example of one such project is Minato Mirai 21 in Yokohama, a port city of over 3 million population, located approximately twenty miles from Tokyo. The Minato Mirai 21 project, slated for completion in the year 2000, is intended to connect and integrate the two major districts of Yokohama, Kannai/Isezakicho and Yokohama Station. It is intended as a new city and will include all the elements of a city system: residences, offices, commercial and public facilities, parks, and so forth. It will cover approximately 460 acres and is projected to cost ¥2 trillion (Yokohama City 1987).

Fifty percent of the common stock in this development project is owned by private enterprise, and the other 50 percent is held by public entities. This type of arrangement is often described as the third sector by Japanese development officials. Included among the private investors are Mitsubishi Estate Company, Mitsubishi Heavy Industries, and the Bank of Yokohama. Public investors include the City of Yokohama, the prefecture, and the Housing and Urban Development Corporation (HUDC).

The vehicle for this public-private partnership is the Yokohama Minato Mirai 21 Corporation, which was established in 1984 to begin promoting the project. The corporation engages in such activities as generating publicity for the project, organizing promotional events inducing businesses to locate in the project, and looking into the development of facilities with communitywide appeal and benefit, based upon good planning and design principles (Hamlin and Lyons 1989).

Multiple Classes of Common Stock. Common stock can be organized into multiple classes (class A, class B, etc.) While all common stock is equally subordinate to all senior securities, each class may have its own set of rights and privileges. Often, equity injections by public or quasipublic sources or equity kickers consist of stock purchases in a class separate from other investors. This separate class may be nonvoting, for example, or may elect a nonvoting representative to the board of directors. In this way it is easier for the public entity to extricate itself from the corporation's business after the public policy goal has been accomplished.

Preferred Stock. Preferred stock is also a security, or written document, representing ownership in a corporation, but is senior to common stock (Ammer and Ammer 1984). This means that should the corporation be forced to go out of business, preferred stockholders would be the first shareholders to be paid from remaining assets. This reduces risk to the preferred shareholders. Dividend rates for preferred stockholders are normally established by the corporation's board of directors and are paid ahead of dividends for common stockholders (Ammer and Ammer 1984). Dividends are more fixed and more closely resemble the interest on debt. In some cases, quasipublic entities purchase preferred stock as an incentive for the appropriate development of a private corporation. In this way, the public sector increases its leverage of private investment capital because of the more positive effect of equity on the balance sheet, while sustaining less risk than if it purchased common stock. Government also maintains a low profile in corporate decisions by not having a voting interest (Lyons and Hamlin 1991).

There are several types of preferred stock that treat dividend payments in different ways. A governmental or quasigovernmental entity will choose from among these, depending on how it wants to participate in the project. (See Ammer and Ammer 1984, p. 361, or Lyons and Hamlin 1991, p. 99, for more details.)

The existence of public-private partnerships has led a new kind of preferred stock to emerge. The governmental or quasigovernmental organization using equity injections usually is concerned only with inducing development. It has no desire to maintain long-term ownership in the company. Therefore, it may buy preferred stock with an agreement that the company will buy the stock back over time. Since the preferred stock pays a regular dividend, and since the periodic repurchase is built into the deal, the security behaves, from the government's point of view, as if it were a loan. From the perspective of the private firm, it provides the equity advantages to the balance sheet discussed earlier in this section. Normally, nonparticipating, noncumulative preferred stock is used (Lyons and Hamlin 1991).

Convertible Securities. Convertible preferred stock has the characteristics of preferred stock described above but also allows the stockholder to exchange it for a specified number of shares of common stock. This type of preferred stock carries a higher risk than other preferred stock because its price is based in part on the price of common stock. If the company, or a particular development, is highly successful, the convertible clause will cause the price of the preferred stock to rise, following the price of the common stock.

Convertible bonds are arguably another form of equity capital. Much like convertible preferred stock, the bondholder is permitted to exchange bonds for common stock at a specified time and price (Ammer and Ammer 1984). While these bonds are technically a form of debt capital, the convertibility provision causes the price of the bond to be based partly on the price of the common stock, thus increasing both the risk and the reward. When an investing government elects to purchase convertible debt, it is, in essence, agreeing to risk greater loss of value for the opportunity to realize a greater return on investment (NASDA, CUED, and the Urban Institute 1983). The convertibility provision creates a kind of equity kicker.

Royalty Agreements. Royalty agreements operate similarly to stock, except that as repayment the holder receives a fixed percentage of the profits realized through the sale of the given firm's product(s). There is usually a maximum royalty. The advantage of royalty agreements is that the govern-ment receives a fixed repayment while the private firm enjoys increased flexibility in the timing and amount of payments (NASDA, CUED, and the Urban Institute 1983).

Warrants. Warrants are contracts that permit the holder, at its option, to buy a fixed number of shares in a given private firm at a fixed price for a limited period of time. They operate much like a call option. Public and quasipublic lenders often accept warrants as an equity kicker attached to a loan deal. If the shares' value surpasses the price established in the warrant during its term, the public warrant holder can exercise its option to buy shares at the fixed price. It then either hold the shares and continues to participate in ownership or sells them and receives a capital gain. In return, the public-sector lender often gives good terms on debt financing to the firm in question (NASDA, CUED, and the Urban Institute 1983).

Limited Partnership Units and Preference Units. If a project is organ-ized as a limited partnership (as described in the section on organizational structures), the local development authority can inject equity into the project by purchasing some of the outstanding units. As a limited partner, the authority would receive a share of profits. Limited partnership preference units give the limited partner first preference over general partners in the payment of any profits. There also may be a limit on the payout to limited partners. This kind of equity instrument behaves much like preferred stock in the way that profits are distributed and risk is experienced, except that the payout qualifies for the same tax advantages as other limited partnership profits. Investors who desire real estate income to offset paper losses from other real estate investments might be interested in the high yield generally offered by these investments.

Indirect Equity Injections

For government to purchase equities directly is sometimes awkward. Often governments act to induce other organizations to provide equity capital. An example of this approach is the Small Business Investment Corporation (SBIC) program, in which the U.S. government gives loans on favorable terms to specially constituted corporations if they agree to make venture capital investments with that money. These SBICs can be for profit or nonprofit, and typically purchase a controlling interest in a new small business or technology. If the technology succeeds, the SBIC sells its share at a substantial profit, perhaps up to 200 percent gain in three years. These proceeds are used to pay off the government loan and reinvest in other ventures (Lyons and Hamlin 1991).

Some public entities have used a small portion of a government employer pension pool as a venture capital fund. The state of Michigan, for example, allows up to 5 percent of the state employees' pension fund to be diverted into a venture capital pool. Since pension funds are often large, a small percentage of a fund can create an enormous venture capital pool. The Michigan Venture Capital Program attempts to use its capital to leverage other private venture capitalists to participate, so as to minimize the pension fund's own risk exposure (Lyons and Hamlin 1991).

Pre-venture capital is another financing need that is often difficult to meet. Pre-venture capital finances research and development at the product development stage, at which new scientific discoveries are translated into marketable products. Without adequate pre-venture capital, many high-tech products would never make it out of the laboratory. Pre-venture capitalists do not buy stock in or control of companies so much as they buy securities that allow them to participate in product success, such as patents, product development rights, and warrants. Pre-venture investments are smaller than venture capital investments but are even more risky. Also, since the investment comes at an early stage of product development, pre-venture capitalists need to be more patient. Foundations and the development funds of public and private universities are supplying pre-venture capital, either directly or by partnering with venture capital firms. Some universities have become involved because they are looking for ways to spin off new products developed in their laboratories. They often want to place new companies in university-sponsored research and industrial parks.

Direct Subsidies

Local and state governments, or private foundations, may offer direct subsidies to private firms to encourage their investment in a renewal area. A direct subsidy is a grant of money made to a private entity without provision for repayment. In most cases such subsidies are tied to efforts by the government to leverage private investment in the area targeted for redevelopment. Economic leveraging, like the word from which it is derived, means making large-scale private investment happen with a minimal initial, or "seed," investment by the public sector (Lyons and Hamlin 1991).

Direct subsidies for urban revitalization generally come in two forms: government grants and private foundation grants. These grants are made with the intent of influencing firms' behavior with regard to investment in new and existing facilities within the renewal area. It is hoped that this direct investment will spur further private investment as revitalization begins to take place. There are several ways that this kind of activity can be leveraged. Two examples are offered in illustration (Lyons and Hamlin 1991).

The first example pertains to the rehabilitation of low-income housing units in city neighborhoods nationwide. An organization known as the Local Initiatives Support Corporation (LISC) makes grants and low-interest loans to community development organizations for the rehabilitation of housing units for low- and moderate-income families. LISC was originally funded by a grant from the Ford Foundation, which it has used to leverage backing from major corporations, government agencies, and other foundations. The grants and loans made by LISC are used to leverage further investment in a specific project, or an entire neighborhood, by private lending institutions (Cook 1987). Among LISC's successes are the rehabilitation of 85 apartment units in New York City's blighted South Bronx neighborhood and the construction of 183 units of housing for moderate-income families in the Hough area of Cleveland (Cook 1987). Often these successes beget further redevelopment, as visual blight is eliminated and private investors' images of the area change for the better.

The other example comes from Indianapolis, Indiana, which has been successful in leveraging central city redevelopment through the improvement of the local quality of life. For many years Indianapolis suffered from the image of a nondescript, if not undesirable, city. It was mocked as "Naptown" and "Indiana No Place." During the 1970s, the city lost 45,000 residents and thousands of jobs (Bamberger and Parham 1984). Indianapolis needed a strategy to counteract this decline, and elected to depart from traditional economic development approaches to accomplish this. The city hit upon the idea of becoming a sports capital and using the notoriety and prestige generated by this activity to leverage further development.

The first sports facility built was Market Square Arena, a basketball and hockey facility completed in 1974. It was constructed using general revenue-sharing funds (Bamberger and Parham 1984). Ten years later, the Hoosierdome, a 61,000-seat indoor football facility, was completed. It was funded through grants from two major private foundations and a 1 percent food and beverage tax (Bamberger and Parham 1984). The city also has constructed a world-class natatorium and track and field facilities near the downtown area, as well as one of the few velodromes in the United States (Bamberger and Parham 1984). These facilities have attracted major sporting events, and the revenues they bring with them, to the city. These events include the 1987 Pan American Games, the 1988 Olympic trials in several events, and a host of major college and professional sporting events.

The new amenities developed by public-private partnerships in Indianapolis have not been limited to sports facilities. The old Circle Theater downtown has been rehabilitated for use by the Indianapolis Symphony Orchestra, the former Indiana Theater has been renovated to house the Indiana Repertory Theater, and the convention center has been expanded and linked to the Hoosierdome to accommodate very large convention groups (Bamberger and Parham 1984).

What kinds of central city development have been leveraged by these investments in amenity infrastructure? Several major hotels have been opened in the downtown in the past several years, including the Union Station Holiday Inn, the Embassy Suites, the Canterbury, the Westin, and the Omni Severn (a rehabilitation of the old Atkinson Hotel). City officials have estimated that in the mid-1980s, new restaurants were opening in the downtown area at the rate of one per month. The city's Union Station has been renovated and adapted for use as a retail/hotel complex. Several major office buildings have been constructed, including the American United Life Building, the Market Tower, the twin-towered Capital Center, and the Bank One Center. New housing is being constructed in the downtown area, and the old Lockerbie Square residential neighborhood, just east of the downtown, has been revitalized, as people are moving back into the central city. The enhanced quality of life has attracted several major corporations and organizations to relocate to Indianapolis, including the Dana Corporation, Purolator Courier, Overland Express, and the Hudson Institute (Bamberger and Parham 1984). All of this private development activity was leveraged by the investment on the part of the city and its charitable organizations in the local amenity infrastructure.

The Japanese government uses a variety of grants to developers to induce them to act within the general constraints of master planning. For example, under the "soft project" system, a particular high-density project area of 200 acres may have a detailed master plan developed for it, and the master plan may call for the construction of housing. Instead of using a government agency such as HUDC to buy out the total project area and redevelop it, the redevelopment agency will redevelop only part of the area. The rest will be put into the incentive system. The incentive system says that if a landowner is willing to redevelop his or her property in strict conformance with the master plan, then the government will give him or her a grant of ¥2 million per housing unit constructed as a cost-reduction incentive. This amounts to about 10 percent of the cost of the average housing unit.

Management

Business Development Assistance

Increasingly, the focus of local economic development efforts has been on the creation of new enterprises. This approach is locally sustainable and recognizes the important role that small businesses play in job creation (see Chapter 6 for a further discussion). Many of the entrepreneurs who start new businesses are idea people and/or technical experts who have very little knowledge of the day-to-day operations of a business. Indeed, poor management is one of the leading causes of the high rate of failure among new businesses. In response, many local communities have developed programs to provide management and business development assistance to their entrepreneurs. Some of these programs take the form of Small Business Development Centers (SBDCs), business incubation programs (see Chapter 6), and entrepreneurship training courses. They typically involve participation by local Chambers of Commerce, the Service Corps of Retired Executives (SCORE), local banks, universities and community colleges, and other public, private, and nonprofit organizations.

No matter what their specific structure, all of these business development programs attempt to school entrepreneurs in basic business management skills: finance, budgeting, human resource development, strategic planning, and related subjects. The entrepreneurs' education may take the form of formal training sessions, workshops, seminars, mentoring, and one-on-one consultation. A thriving small business sector is recognized to be in the entire community's best interest.

Feasibility Studies

Public agencies can offer a valuable incentive to private development by preparing feasibility studies for individual firms or entire industries. Market studies, financial feasibility analyses, fiscal impact studies, and similar investigations help firms make important decisions (NASDA, CUED, and the Urban Institute 1983). The intention, of course, is to provide the firm or industry with useful information that will enhance its market position and at the same time highlight the assisting locale as a desirable location for investment (Lyons 1987). Often a public body will have better access to this information and a better understanding of how to use it than private companies will (Lyons and Hamlin 1991).

Tax Incentives

Tax incentives are also financial inducements to private development. They are aimed at reducing the cost of doing business by decreasing the tax burden on firms that invest in a targeted renewal area. These incentives afford moratoriums, exemptions, or abatements on the many varieties of taxation encountered by businesses. Among these are corporate income taxes; use taxes; sales taxes; property taxes on land, plant, equipment, and machinery; excise taxes; and payroll taxes (NASDA, CUED, and the Urban Institute 1983). Like the incentives intended to abate them, the taxes levied vary by state and municipality (Lyons 1987).

Exemptions and Abatements

The following represent some of the more commonly used tax incentives (*Site Selection Handbook* 1985):

Special corporate income tax exemptions except the recipient firm(s) from taxation of profits. This incentive is often used to encourage employment of identified types or numbers of workers (NASDA, CUED, and the Urban Institute 1983).

Corporate tax abatements lower the enterprise (or business) taxes levied by the local government in Japan. (they are similar to state single business taxes in the United States.) These taxes can be reduced by the local government as an incentive to development.

Special personal income tax exemptions are similar to corporate income tax exemptions, except that they pertain to individual income. They are most often directed at small business entrepreneurs to encourage them to utilize more labor or capital by exempting them from taxes on portions of their income (Lyons 1987).

Excise tax exemptions apply to excise taxes on the consumption of specific goods levied by some states. They are commonly applied to commodities such as gasoline and other fuels (NASDA, CUED, and the Urban Institute 1983). Excise tax exemptions are intended to reduce operations costs for firms that use large amounts of these commodities (Lyons 1987).

Inventory tax exemptions concern taxes on goods in transit that are, in essence, personal property taxes on items warehoused in the state levying the tax but intended for delivery to another jurisdiction. States may exempt these goods from taxation by giving them "free port" status (NASDA, CUED, and the Urban Institute 1983).

Manufacturers' inventory tax exemptions release firms that store items for use in the production process from paying this form of personal property tax levied by some states. These exemptions are normally reserved for certain specified inventory (Lyons 1987).

Tax exemptions or moratoriums on land/capital improvements and on equipment and machinery are very specific types of tax incentives. They seek to encourage investment in land and capital equipment by exempting firms from property taxes on these production inputs, either indefinitely or for an established time period (Lyons 1987). The government offering these incentives does so in the hope that the resultant expansion in capital investment will be accompanied by an increase in labor input as well (Lyons 1987). Governments contemplating use of these incentives for generating new jobs should be aware that they can have a perverse impact on job creation. That is, a reduction in the cost of capital may encourage a firm to employ more capital at the expense of labor, depending upon the firm's elasticity of demand for labor.

Sales and use tax exemptions on new capital equipment are fairly common tax incentives. Sales taxes are borne by the purchaser and are levied on goods sold at retail or wholesale. Use taxes are imposed on the use, consumption, or storage of items not subject to a sales tax (NASDA, CUED, and the Urban Institute 1983). Exemptions from these taxes seek to stimulate capital expansion on the part of private recipients (Lyons 1987).

Tax stabilization agreements are another incentive used to attract investment by certain specified industries. These agreements often embody a commitment by the government to limit fluctuations in the amount and type of taxation borne by the selected private-sector beneficiaries (Lyons 1987).

Tax exemptions to encourage research and development represent an increasingly popular form of tax incentive. Greater emphasis on advanced technologies in industry should cause this incentive to continue to grow in importance (Lyons 1987). The taxes most often included in these exemptions are property taxes, the corporate income tax, and sales and use taxes that impact firms conducting research and development (NASDA, CUED, and the Urban Institute 1983).

Accelerated depreciation of capital equipment is an indirect tax incentive. This inducement operates on the theory that a firm that can reduce its property tax liability by depreciating its equipment at a faster rate will reinvest those savings in the expansion of its facilities (Lyons 1987). Like the U.S. public sector, the Japanese government offers accelerated depreciation on capital equipment for tax purposes. In exchange, the firm availing itself of this incentive agrees to cooperate with the HUDC in its redevelopment endeavors.

Tax credits for training the "chronically" unemployed seek to encourage businesses to invest in training for this segment of the labor force. This incentive is often targeted at large manufacturing or service businesses that employ sizable numbers of semiskilled and unskilled workers (Lyons 1987).

Toka-Kocan system is employed in Japan, where land values are so high that most development incentive programs tend to be aimed at mitigating this problem or avoiding taxation when land changes hands. *Toka-Kocan*, or equivalent value exchange, is one such incentive. It allows for the legal trade of real estate with no sales or capital gains taxes. The land is then owned by the developer and the original landowner in some proportion (e.g., 65 percent owned by developer, 35 percent owned by original owner). The relationship between the two parties is a partnership of sorts, but the original landowner bears no liability.

Enterprise Zones

Enterprise zones represent another type of development inducement employing tax incentives. The concept of the enterprise zone was originally developed in Great Britain by Peter Hall, and was aimed at freeing private businesses, located within certain geographic areas, from government regulation (Sidor 1982, pp. 1–2). This approach has been adjusted in the United States to consist of the designation of low-income, high-unemployment urban areas for redevelopment. Within these zones, economic revitalization is encouraged via a package of tax incentives that is intended to stimulate development and, hence, the creation of new jobs (Sidor 1982). Several states in the United States have adopted enterprise zone legislation. There is considerable variation in zone size, eligibility requirements, and zone incentives across the states, making it difficult to generalize about the nature of these entities (Sidor 1982).

In concept, enterprise zones also employ the relaxation of some development regulations as a further incentive to development within the zone. In practice, this feature is controversial and legally complex, although the incentives built into land use laws can be emphasized within the zone (Lyons and Hamlin 1991). A somewhat modified version of the enterprise zone concept has been formulated by the Clinton administration in the United States, with the name "empowerment zone."

The Japanese government is considering enterprise zone legislation, but their enterprise zone is more of a bonus zoning concept than it is a business development concept. A revision in the current law would allow HUDC projects to increase their floor area ratio in certain areas of the city where population decline is a problem and housing is included in a carefully planned renewal project.

Tax Increment Financing

Tax increment financing (TIF) combines the elements of several of the public-private partnership activities discussed in this book. This development financing technique is commonly used to spur redevelopment in deteriorated urban areas. The unique aspect of TIF is that, from the public-sector standpoint, the cost of inducing development is borne by all the taxing jurisdictions affecting the redevelopment area in proportion to the increase in property tax revenues they receive as a result of redevelopment (Huddleston 1981).

In order for a city to engage in TIF, the state in which it is located must have enacted specific enabling legislation. The particulars of this legislation vary from state to state but follow a basic form. The city begins by establishing a TIF district. This may range in size from a single city block to an entire central business district. The city is normally required to prepare an inventory of the land uses, zoning, and building stock for the district and a redevelopment plan for approval before the TIF process can proceed. Assessments for the district are frozen at their present value (American Planning Association 1976). This affects all taxing jurisdictions that include the designated TIF district. The combined assessed valuation of all the property in the TIF district is the "base value" of the district (Lyons and Hamlin 1991).

The city, through its tax increment finance authority (TIFA), can acquire land and make capital improvements in the district (e.g., streets, lighting, landscaping, etc.) to make it more desirable to developers. It also can offer additional incentives to private development in the area of the kinds discussed in this chapter. When development occurs, the value of the real property in the district increases. This increased value is taxed, but for the period of time during which the TIF district is in effect, the tax revenues resulting from the increment in value go to the TIFA, not the other taxing jurisdictions. These additional taxes not distributed to other taxing jurisdictions are the tax increment. The TIFA uses the tax increment to pay off the expenses incurred by the city in land acquisition and the installation of capital improvements (Huddleston 1981). (For an example to illustrate how TIF works see, Lyons and Hamlin 1991, p. 108, or Huddleston 1981, pp. 374–376.)

Markets

Market Stabilization

One way for the public sector to induce the private sector to act in desired ways is for the government to be a guaranteed buyer of the private sector's product. A real estate example of this is the situation where government, in exchange for desired developer behavior, promises to rent some portion of a development project for a guaranteed period of time at an agreed-upon price. If the local municipality needs to expand its city hall floor area, for example, one approach might be to rent space from the private sector rather than to build a new government building. This can be a real plum to offer a developer of a project who is willing to cooperate by developing according to the plan of the city. Even if the city rents only a small portion of an office building project, the resulting income stability can significantly reduce the risk of the project for the developer.

From the public side, the city obtains the space it needs while promoting the development of a desirable project. At first this approach appears expensive because the city must pay rent over many years rather than own its own building. On the other hand, the city receives the tax revenues from the completed building and avoids some or all of the expense of a new city hall, including debt costs. Depending on the rent it negotiates, the city may actually save money.

If an office tower were structured as an office condominium, the city could float public purpose tax-exempt general obligation bonds to buy part of the office condo, thus guaranteeing the developer an immediate return on at least part of the investment (Lyons and Hamlin 1991).

Programs to Increase Exports

Governments sometimes provide technical assistance to private firms wishing to market their products internationally (Lyons 1987). This assistance includes information on trade opportunities abroad, help in creating linkages with foreign buyers, assistance in organizing trade shows, guidance in accessing federal export resources, and direct marketing assistance (Long 1984). This incentive can be used by government to encourage firms to locate in declining urban areas and to expand their production—and, hence, their operations. It also can be used as part of a package of inducements to lure private firms into investing in new operations in local communities (Lyons and Hamlin 1991).

Federal Contract Procurement

The federal government in the United States lets numerous contracts to private firms. While defense spending is the largest part of the federal budget, the federal government purchases all kinds of products, from soap to shoes. These contracts can be quite lucrative. Large firms, particularly those that have been awarded contracts previously, have a decided advantage in the competition for new contracts due to their familiarity with the process and better information on contract availability. Governmental assistance in obtaining procurement information, bidding on contracts, and managing contracts can help to spread the benefit of federal procurement to a large base of firms, and induce firms to develop in declining areas (Lyons and Hamlin 1991).

Research

These programs offer research assistance in the form of expert consultation, both public and private, including appropriate faculty from public universities and community colleges. This may be taken a step further by making public university R&D facilities available for use by private firms (Lyons 1987). With the proliferation of urban branches of major state universities since 1970, this incentive becomes particularly useful for promoting central city redevelopment. Many governments collect, retain, disseminate, and update data that are helpful to industrial R&D efforts (Lyons 1987).

Project Coordination Function

Project coordination really amounts to focusing and integrating all of the activities mentioned above in a specifically defined project area. A hypothetical scenario is as follows. First, all land is acquired or the cooperative participation of private property owners is assured. Second, property lines are redrawn to produce more useful parcels and better transportation access. This may involve land readjustment. Third, physical infrastructure improvements are made to modernize the project area and prepare it for development. Fourth, the feasibility of various development alternatives is investigated. A project may require financial or other incentives in order to be feasible (Lyons and Hamlin 1991).

Fifth, publicly owned land is sold to private developers at below market prices if the buyers are willing to develop the project within the planning guidelines. Sixth, other private owners are induced to build in accordance with the project plan because of benefits they receive from property line readjustments, infrastructure improvements, improvements in surrounding developments, labor force training, market stabilization agreements and financial incentives, export promotion, marketing assistance, and the entire package of potential governmental incentive programs.

CHAPTER 5

HANDS: Opening Doors

PUBLIC–PRIVATE PARTNERSHIP FOR COMMUNITY EMPOWERMENT

Housing and Neighborhood Development Strategies (HANDS), an innovative neighborhood revitalization program in Louisville, Kentucky, was created in 1993 under a three-year, $1.5 million grant from the U.S. Department of Education. Operated by the University of Louisville, its mission is to focus its resources and the teaching, research, and community service activities of its faculty on improving the quality of life in its urban context. The university has partnered with other institutions of secondary and higher education, private business, local government, and nonprofit organizations to make HANDS's ongoing work possible, and has received an additional $750,000 in local matching grants, consisting of both cash and in-kind services.

HANDS is the quintessential manifestation of the University of Louisville's mission in the urban redevelopment arena. It links the university's resources to the community's needs, thereby permitting the university to meet its responsibilities as a major stakeholder in the city. The extensive partnership process operating across the spectrum of organizational types makes it a living laboratory of public entrepreneurship and private statesmanship. The purpose of this chapter is to investigate HANDS in the context of the ideas presented in previous chapters, and to view HANDS as an example of extensive intersectoral partnerships in a local economy losing its sectoral walls.

RUSSELL

The focus of HANDS's efforts is the low-income, inner city neighbor-hood on the city's west side known as Russell. To date, it has concentrated most of its efforts in East Russell, that portion of the neighborhood located closest to Louisville's central business district. Plans call for expanding the program's services westward in the near future. Russell has a population of approximately 10,000 and is a historic, largely African-American commu-nity. It has been one of Kentucky's, and one of the nation's, most economi-cally disadvantaged areas. It suffers from high levels of unemployment, poverty, crime, and homelessness. In 1989, Russell's poverty rate was 65 percent, and its median household income was only 27 percent of that of Louisville as a whole. The unemployment rate was approximately 27 percent, including one-third of all youths aged sixteen to nineteen. The high school dropout rate was 57 percent. One-third of the neighborhood's residents were on public assistance.

Despite being near downtown, the community experiences isolation. One-quarter of all of Russell's households do not have a telephone. Two-thirds do not own automobiles. Only 19 percent of the neighborhood's households own their own home. Of these, 29 percent pay more than the federal government's "30 percent of household income" standard on hous-ing costs. Among Russell's renters, 51 percent pay in excess of the federal standard. Yet neighborhood housing suffers a 21 percent vacancy rate. Local community service agencies maintain that these figures are conservative, and that the community's underclass is much larger and its problems even greater (Gilderbloom et al. 1994; Gilderbloom and Mullins 1994).

Physically, Russell is comprised of a mixture of land uses. It is largely residential in nature, with both single-family and multiple-family units. In addition, it contains commercial, industrial, and public institutional uses. Among commercial uses, grocery stores and pharmacies are in short supply. Taverns, liquor stores, and pawnshops abound. Abandoned housing dots the neighborhood. Many structures have already been razed, leaving entire blocks vacant (Gilderbloom and Mullins 1994).

Russell is a neighborhood where the partnership of public and private goals necessary to sustain a community in a free market system broke down. Government did not maintain the stability necessary for the free market to work. Externalities associated with an aging infrastructure, deteriorating housing stock, incompatible land use patterns, and antiquated lot subdivisions have complicated redevelopment and frustrated the natural process of urban renewal. Concentrations of disadvantaged individuals leading to social disor-

ganization increased investment risk and frightened away financial intermediaries. Some say that insensitive urban renewal programs of previous decades overemphasized housing clearance. They damaged the social fabric of
the community and strained trust in government. In a classic case of inner city
market failure, a downward spiral ensued, and private investment pulled out,
exacerbating the isolation and hopelessness of remaining residents.

Despite all of the above, Russell's unique assets afford the potential to
reverse the downward spiral. They may restore a situation where market
forces can again promote the natural process of urban renewal. One of
Russell's assets is its heritage. The neighborhood has a long history as the
locus of African-American cultural, social, residential, and economic activity
in Louisville. Originally established as a white, upper-income, Victorian
neighborhood, it became predominantly African-American as early as 1925
(Louisville and Jefferson County Planning Commission 1984). Some black
institutions in the neighborhood precede that date. Plymouth Congregational
Church was founded in 1880 on the site it currently occupies. The first public
library in the country created exclusively for the black community was built
in Russell in 1908. The neighborhood has been home to several locally and
nationally prominent African-American figures, including educator Harvey
Clarence Russell (for whom the community is named), architect Samuel
Plato, artist Burt Hurley, and author and poet Joseph Cotter (Louisville and
Jefferson County Planning Commission 1984). In May 1980, much of Russell
was placed on the National Register of Historic Places as a historic district
(Louisville and Jefferson County Planning Commission 1984).

This social and cultural heritage has helped the community maintain its
identity and a core of loyal residents during a difficult period of its history.
Crime data may be revealing of the strength of this social fabric, since
Russell's crime rate has actually dropped 10 percent since 1990. During the
same time period, adjoining neighborhoods have experienced increases in
their crime rates of up to 69 percent.

While the Russell neighborhood experienced long-term decline, market
failure, and downward spiral, its social assets made it a candidate for
economic reversal. Hope emerged that the proper collaboration of public
and private forces might solve personal and social problems, mitigate
market imperfections, and restore the natural process of urban renewal.
People also recognized, through the input received from citizens, that a
focused, comprehensive approach to neighborhood revitalization would be
required. It would need to address personal problems of citizens and
families, social issues, micro- and macroeconomic factors, and the condition of the public and private physical infrastructure. Any gap in this

approach would be the weakest link in a chain of events required to lift the entire neighborhood out of troubled waters.

It was also clear that large amounts of public funds were not available at any level. Rejuvenation of the Russell neighborhood would necessitate an array of organizations interlinked with a system of collaborative associations. This effort would require every kind of organization on the public–private spectrum, each with its own mission, expertise, legal powers, cadre of leaders, and sources of public and private investment capital. It would mean coming to a consensus about the public policy interests of the neighborhood through careful, sensitive communication with local citizens and political leaders. At the same time an environment attractive to private investment would be essential.

Initially, public and quasipublic agents in the community began to change their attitudes and their policies toward Russell. Several years ago, the city urban renewal agency began an approach to neighborhood preservation that deemphasized clearance, and put greater importance on citizen involvement. In addition to much of Russell being placed on the National Register of Historic Places, the core residential district has been designated by the city of Louisville as a Community Development Neighborhood Strategy Area, making it eligible for federal housing rehabilitation funds. These developments were complemented by the creation of the non-profit Russell Neighborhood Commercial Revitalization and Development Corporation, which sponsors a program for the acquisition, renovation, and resale of substandard housing units (Gilderbloom et al. 1994).

The city of Louisville has budgeted approximately $900,000 in rehabilitation programs and $1.1 million in public improvements for Russell. It spent $10 million on the development of Hampton Place, a 150-unit rental project. The city's community housing development corporation has designated Russell as eligible for $600,000 to build new single-family housing units for households that earn $27,000/year or less. Russell is also eligible to take advantage of a citywide homestead program.

As a result of this investment, and that of other entities, Russell has recently seen the construction of 150 middle-income rental housing units by the city, 24 single-family units by Habitat for Humanity, 8 houses by the Louisville Central Development Corporation, and 8 houses by the Urban League Rebound Program, and the rehabilitation of 40 units by other developers; plans for 180 more units are on the drawing board.

Thus, while the neighborhood suffers from serious social and economic problems, it also has the social support infrastructure that gives it the degree of stability necessary to make its revitalization possible (Gilderbloom et al. 1994).

The Creation of HANDS

As momentum for rejuvenation of Russell began to build, in stepped a key actor in the welfare of the entire metropolitan area, the University of Louisville. HANDS had its genesis in the circulation of a request for proposals issued by the U.S. Department of Education for its Urban Community Services Program in January 1992. A small group from the University of Louisville, headed by Dr. John Gilderbloom of the university's Center for Urban and Economic Research, submitted a proposal that caught the Department of Education's attention. It proposed a comprehensive approach to inner city revitalization.

The results of a number of surveys taken in Louisville in recent years indicated that housing and neighborhood revitalization were two of the most pressing issues facing that city (Durbin 1992). Residents deemed housing affordability most important. Statistics indicate that the city has a substantial housing problem. Nationwide, one of every twenty houses is substandard. In some Louisville neighborhoods, the figure is one in four. Most low-income renters pay in excess of 50 percent of their income for housing. Within the city of Louisville proper, 13 percent of multiple-family housing units and 12 percent of single-family units are substandard. Over 12,000 persons requested emergency shelter in Louisville in 1991. Louisville mayor, Jerry Abramson, president of the U.S. Conference of Mayors, has made addressing the related problems of affordable housing and neighborhood revitalization one of his administration's top priorities (Gilderbloom et al. 1994).

Recognizing that the housing crisis cannot be blamed solely on a lack of affordable housing (Lowry 1992; Gilderbloom, et al. 1992), and that piecemeal efforts are doomed to failure, HANDS proposed a multifaceted approach to the problems of housing and neighborhood deterioration being experienced in Louisville. The HANDS strategy includes a synergistic combination of job development, education, leadership training, community planning and design, home ownership programs, entrepreneurship training, and loan programs (Gilderbloom et al. 1994).

In many respects the real impetus for putting together HANDS was the effort by a local group, Leadership Louisville, to establish a fellows program, using a $500,000 donation from the Mary and Barry Bingham, Sr., Foundation. The purpose of the program was to identify a major community problem, analyze it, develop alternatives for its solution, and generate a plan for implementing these solutions. The Bingham fellows chose affordable housing as the problem they would address, and made their goal "to make affordable, safe, and decent housing available to every person in the Louisville metropolitan area by the year 1995" (Gilderbloom et al. 1994).

The Bingham fellows formed the Housing Partnership, Inc., in July 1990. This private, nonprofit partnership among local governments, individual civic leaders, and major corporations was assembled to coordinate the affordable housing effort in metropolitan Louisville. The focus was on enabling home ownership, which was seen as the key to economic stability (Gilderbloom et al. 1994).

From January to July 1992, serious consideration was given to ways in which the proposal for the Urban Community Service Grant might use the Bingham fellows' efforts as a basis for further work in housing and community revitalization in Louisville. Over 200 hours of meetings with various organizations and community leaders were held during this period. One such meeting involved the presidents of the city's seven largest banks, local Realtors, and major local architectural firms. In addition, four versions of the grant proposal were circulated to over 100 individuals and organizations, soliciting their input. Based on this communitywide participation and feedback, HANDS was born as an innovative, yet pragmatic, partnership (Gilderbloom et al. 1994).

The "Partners" in HANDS

An active and extensive collaboration of public, private, and nonprofit entities within and outside of Louisville developed HANDS and sustains it. The groups represent the spectrum of organizational types increasingly found in the economy without walls. These partners fall into several categories: the University of Louisville, a public institution; various government and quasigovernmental entities; community-based organizations; churches; public schools; and national and community advisory teams.

Aspects of the university's role in the partnership are worthy of detailed examination. One has to do with how unusual it is for a major university to play an active, multifaceted part in a comprehensive community empowerment and revitalization effort like this one. Examples of institutions of higher education providing training, or some other single function, to a revitalization effort abound. Universities that take the lead in individual projects are relatively common as well. Seldom, however, is a university's participation this broad-based.

The University of Louisville's role as both leader and facilitator of the Russell neighborhood's revitalization, through the HANDS project, also is unique. Every successful public–private partnership has strong leadership from one or more of the partners. The university plays this important part in Russell. Furthermore, the University, by virtue of its perceived neutral, objective stance, has been in a position to bring diverse parties and their resources to the partnership in relative harmony.

Government Partners

The two principal local government partners in the Russell revitalization effort are the city of Louisville and Jefferson County. Participating branches and agencies of the city include the Mayor's Office, the Board of Aldermen, the Department of Housing and Urban Development, the Housing Authority of Louisville, and the Division of Police. County government participants include the Office of Economic Development. The HANDS Community Advisory Team includes five members from local government, among them a member of the city's Board of Aldermen (Gilderbloom et al. 1994).

Community-Based Organizations

Community-based organizations are vital collaborators in the Russell renaissance. Members of several of these groups serve on the HANDS Community Advisory Team. Participating organizations include those based in Russell and those that have a broader community- or citywide interest. Examples of the former are Plymouth Community Center, which makes its facilities available for meetings, seminars, and workshops, and the Russell Area Council. Organizations with a broader base include housing providers, such as Habitat for Humanity, Housing Partnership Inc., and the Metro Housing Coalition; Louisville Central Community Centers; Louisville Central Development Corporation, which engages in housing and economic development activities; the Louisville Urban League; and West Louisville Ministries (Gilderbloom et al. 1994). Several of these organizations are themselves intersectoral partnerships that receive governmental and private-sector funding and guidance.

National governmental participation involves the U.S. Department of Education and the U.S. Housing and Urban Development Department. Returned Peace Corps fellows also are working in the area.

Churches

Local churches play a very strong role in Russell and in the HANDS partnership. The Russell neighborhood has nearly fifty churches, an average of about one church for every 200 residents. Many longtime Russell residents who left their neighborhood during the period of rapid deterioration maintained their emotional ties through continued participation in local churches. Some of these families are proving to be a part of the market for middle-income housing now being built there. HANDS has held numerous meetings at neighborhood churches, and its staff has made presentations at Sunday services on several occasions. Local pastors provide considerable input and feedback to the HANDS effort (Gilderbloom et al. 1994).

Schools

The Jefferson County public schools represent another important partner in the HANDS undertaking. Four public schools, including three elementary schools—Byck, Coleridge-Taylor, and Roosevelt-Perry—are situated within the neighborhood. The Russell neighborhood is also home to Louisville Central High School. Coleridge-Taylor Elementary School is the site of a family resources center sponsored by HANDS. To date, eighty students have enrolled in the esteem training programs that are conducted there (Gilderbloom et al. 1994).

National and Community Advisory Teams

Two advisory groups have been established to provide guidance to the community empowerment effort in Russell: a community advisory team and a national advisory team. The purpose of both groups is to assist with all-important monitoring and evaluation activities. HANDS makes use of the information emanating from this process, and from other sources, to assess the effectiveness of the various elements of the overall effort in Russell. It has employed this knowledge to reassess program goals and objectives, effect necessary personnel changes, and terminate all, or parts, of certain programs.

The community advisory team includes Russell residents and leaders from government, labor, banking, and housing organizations that serve the area. This useful mix of clients and technical experts brings their individual perspectives to the evaluation of HANDS programs. The national advisory team, a collection of experts in aspects of community empowerment and revitalization, includes Derek Bok of Harvard University; author Mark Dowie; Roger E. Hamlin of Michigan State University; Vincent Lane, chairman of the Chicago Housing Authority; Marilyn Melkonian, president of Telesis Corporation; and I. Donald Terner, president of Bridge Housing Corporation in San Francisco (Gilderbloom et al. 1994).

HANDS Activities

Activities of the HANDS partnership in the Russell neighborhood fall into several major categories: job training, entrepreneurship assistance, education, leadership training, case management, home ownership, and community design. This wide-ranging collection of integrated activities is in keeping with the partnership's comprehensive approach to community empowerment and revitalization in Russell. Below we discuss these endeavors by category (Gilderbloom et al. 1994)

Job Training

Job training plays a crucial role in the HANDS approach because of the high levels of unemployment and underemployment in Russell. The job training program, which models itself after a similar program administered by the Louisville Urban League, seeks to prepare participants for skilled jobs that pay between $7 and $12 per hour. The project provides two levels of training: "entry" training, designed for participants with no work history, and "remedial" training, aimed at those with a history of minimum wage employment and outdated job skills. Recipients of remedial training often find that without it, they are unable to compete in the labor market because minimum wage laws tend to increase the reluctance of employers to provide general training to unskilled workers.

The HANDS job training program begins by preparing participants for the world of work. This translates to basic skill-building in the following areas: self-actualization, employability skills and job search techniques, employer expectations, and human relations/interpersonal communications. One example of the type of training delivered is a segment on effective communication skills in the workplace offered by the University of Louisville's Labor Management Center. This training employs a variety of hands-on techniques, including role-playing, to prepare participants for this highly important aspect of work life.

Another aspect of job training via the HANDS program is mentoring for unemployed and underemployed adults. The project assigns each job trainee to a local leader in labor or management relations who serves as that individual's mentor. Mentors are selected for their knowledge of the necessary skills for success in the modern workplace. They provide one-on-one attention to the skill-building needs of the trainees.

The computer skills course is another example of the types of training provided. Trainees from both the Russell and the LaSalle neighborhoods received eight weeks of hands-on training in using business computer

systems. The course covered skills such as understanding computer termi-
nology, using word-processing software, developing typing speed, using
spreadsheets, entering alpha and numeric data, and understanding the skills
that will be required in the future, based on trends in computer software use.
Recent graduates of this course have found positions with major local
employers, including the American Red Cross, Cumberland Bank, Humana,
and Louisville Gas & Electric.

Entrepreneurship Assistance

Preparing and assisting Russell residents who are interested in starting
their own businesses is another strategy used by HANDS to encourage
community revitalization. The intent is to create homegrown firms that will
bring jobs, income, and local investment back to the community. Four
specific actions are employed: an entrepreneurship training course, a business micro-loan program, a business incubation program, and a minority
business directory.

The entrepreneurship course covers an eight-week period. It focuses on
empowerment and instilling a spirit of self-sufficiency in participants.
Specifically, the training includes segments on identifying viable markets,
business plan development, capital acquisition, marketing, finance and
bookkeeping, business networking, and strategic planning. Mentoring by
successful African-American business people is part of the program.

A second action used to encourage entrepreneurship is a business micro-
loan program. The program used is the Louisville Central Community
Centers, Inc./City of Louisville Business Plus Microloan Program. It is
designed to be an alternative source of seed capital to traditional lending
institutions, which are reluctant to lend to high-risk small businesses whose
owners may have no collateral and either no credit history or a poor one.
The Microloan Program employs peer lending groups to make small loans
with no requirement of collateral or credit history. Applicants must submit
a business plan to a peer group for approval. A manager is designated to
oversee the operations of the peer groups. The program provides applicants
with a four-to-six week orientation program that is designed to bring them
up to speed on financial management and business planning.

The business incubation program to be offered by HANDS consists of
the development of a small-scale residential incubator that offers low-cost
space, shared office support services, management assistance, and access
to the business micro-loan program. The incubation period for the incubator
clients is projected to be six to nine months. To date, the incubator has not
begun operation.

The final part of HANDS's entrepreneurship assistance strategy is the development of a minority business directory, in collaboration with the Louisville and Jefferson County Office of Economic Development. The purpose of the directory is to make information on local minority firms and their products and services available to larger corporations that may be looking for suppliers. It serves to give community minority businesses a higher profile, with the hope that this will ultimately increase their sales.

Education

Perhaps more basic than job training and entrepreneurship training to the success of the HANDS community empowerment effort in Russell is education. Education prepares the individual to be trained for work. It brings with it employment for the unemployed, a chance at well-paying jobs for the underemployed, higher earning potential for all, and an increased opportunity for home ownership.

The School of Education at the University of Louisville plays an instrumental role in developing and delivering a comprehensive program of education to Russell residents. The training delivery system makes use of the school's new teacher education program. The program has four components: Adults and Children Coordinated Education (ACCE); Pooling Assets for Continuing Educational Development (PACED), Literacy is a Family Affair (LAFA), and Community Teaching and Tutoring (CTT).

ACCE helps local youth and adults to complete their high school education and earn the Graduate Equivalency Diploma (GED). Accredited courses aimed at this objective are offered in community centers located in the neighborhood. Jefferson County's Adult and Continuing Education Program provides these and other continuing education courses.

PACED is designed to pick up where ACCE leaves off, by expanding opportunities for local youth and adults to attend college or other educational or vocational training programs, after completing high school. The partner in this effort, Kentuckiana Metrouniversity, gives financial aid to Russell residents who wish to continue their education. Scholarships are solicited from private foundations and corporations. Metrouniversity staff also offer counseling services and workshops for residents to explore various educational avenues.

Another program important to the HANDS educational effort is LAFA, implemented with the National Center for Family Literacy. LAFA brings parents and children together in the educational process. As they attend school together, parents get closer to their children and instill in them an appreciation for the value and importance of education. Thus, the program yields literate parents and children, empowered to move to higher levels of educational achievement. Early studies of family literacy programs show that 90 percent of the children who participate go on to enjoy success in school. LAFA operates in both the Russell and the neighboring LaSalle communities.

The University of Louisville School of Education requires its students to provide a specified number of hours of service to the community in order to graduate. It has partnered with HANDS to provide the CTT program to residents of Russell. CTT trains residents in basic job skills, remedial education, and grade school and high school programs. University student interns work directly with residents as their teachers and tutors. A community study hall equipped with computers is provided as part of the program. It provides an environment that is conducive to learning.

Leadership Training

HANDS views local leadership development as crucial to ensuring permanent, high-quality change in the Russell neighborhood. The objective of the HANDS leadership training program is to reinforce and further enhance the capabilities and skills of individuals in the Russell neighborhood who demonstrate an inclination and capacity for leadership. The program has been designed to train 150 participants in traditional community organizing strategies, as well as entrepreneurship and positive lifestyle, career, and financial approaches. It is intended that once the first group of community leaders has been trained, they will train other resident groups. In this way, community leadership will be perpetuated.

The leadership training program is being carried out by a partnership that includes Jefferson County Public Schools, the Louisville Central Community Center, the Louisville Community Design Center, and the University of Louisville's College of Business and Public Administration. The program started with fifteen residents who expressed a desire to work for change in the neighborhood. Among members of this group were small business owners, child-care workers, local religious leaders, and a chef. The group was selected to constitute the first of six leadership classes. The class, which was facilitated by a member of the staff of the Louisville Community Design Center, focused its attention on studying several models for successful organizational development and neighborhood improvement. After two meetings, the group had identified core issues to be addressed in Russell, including improved housing, drug prevention, job opportunities, and parental guidance.

Entrepreneurship has become a principal focus of the leadership training program because project leaders see it as a mechanism for breaking the intergenerational cycle of dependency found in the neighborhood and for providing the economic resources that make the solution of communitywide problems possible. Economic empowerment becomes the vehicle for attaining individual self-sufficiency and, ultimately, communitywide quality of life. With this in mind, HANDS established a community speakers program aimed at enterprise development for African-Americans. In addition, the College of Business and Public Administration at the University of Louisville is organizing an internship program for students earning an MBA degree. The student interns will work with African-American businesspeople. It is expected that the students will serve as resources to the business people and, in return, will learn management, accounting, marketing, and business leadership skills.

Self-esteem is a major prerequisite for leadership. In conjunction with Jefferson County Public Schools, HANDS has formulated an "esteem program" for youth in the Russell neighborhood. It seeks to encourage the young to believe in themselves, their parents, and their community. Self-esteem and respect for others are fostered through various life skills exercises, community service efforts, performing arts activities, and parent involvement.

Case Management

HANDS has an extensive, multidisciplinary case management system. The project creates family advocate skills teams (FASTs) to perform comprehensive family assessments and counsel families living in the Russell target area. This program serves 400 families. A certified social worker coordinates each FAST and is joined by a social work intern, a nursing student, an early childhood specialist, and/or a gerontologist. Team leaders serve as case managers. The duties of a case manager include surveying families, planning with them, and networking them with existing community resources and HANDS programs. These latter resources may include services in employment, education, child care, wellness, home ownership, and other areas. The social work interns who participate in the FASTs are drawn from the social work programs of three local institutions of higher education: the Southern Baptist Seminary, Spalding University, and the University of Louisville. Nursing students come from the University of Louisville and Spalding University.

The case management teams operate in a proactive manner. They make initial appointments with families and visit them in their homes. During these visits, they complete assessments of family needs and desires relative to educational opportunities, employment, and home ownership. To date, FAST teams have contacted all 400 households about their interest and eligibility for home ownership in renovated condominiums in the target area. The FASTs' intervention to connect these families with educational counseling and job training services is crucial to realizing the dream of home ownership, which requires a stable income and good credit. The case management teams have helped with a wide variety of needs. One young local resident wanted to attend a Kentucky junior college on a basketball scholarship. His family's case manager took the student and his mother to the campus for a visit, and arranged for tutoring for the ACT exam to improve his chances of passing. Access to case managers by the families they serve is enhanced by locating the HANDS field office in the heart of the Russell neighborhood.

Home Ownership

HANDS provides a gateway to the Housing Authority of Louisville's home ownership program. Interested Russell families can contact HANDS for an application that, when completed, is reviewed and referred to a housing counselor. The counselor then arranges a meeting with the family and conducts a full analysis of its financial situation to ascertain barriers to mortgage loan approval. The results of the analysis become the basis for a plan of action to help the family become eligible for financing. HANDS places each participating family in one of four groups with financial and credit characteristics similar to their own. In addition, the counselor helps the family calculate the appropriate house price range. Once the family mitigates its identified barriers to home financing (e.g., improved credit standing, an adequate savings account, good money management skills), they enter the educational phase of the program. The counselor assists them throughout this preparatory process.

In the educational phase, qualified participants attend a series of seven lectures covering the home buying process. Lecture topics are credit, home inspection, Realtor selection, sales contracting, mortgage financing, home-owner's insurance, and loan application and closing. Participants receive a certificate of program completion and continue to receive counseling for six months to help them improve their budgeting skills, establish reserve accounts for repair and replacement, and avoid mortgage foreclosure. Program graduates may reenter at any time, should they need to.

Home ownership opportunities in the community have been enhanced through HANDS's partnership with the Housing Authority of Louisville to convert the LaSalle Public Housing Project to condominiums. HANDS's leadership, job education, and home ownership training components were used by the Housing Authority as an in-kind match in the latter's successful application for a $7 million federal grant to effect the conversion. The 150 condominiums are available to low-income, first-time home buyers. Prices range from $18,000 for one-bedroom to $36,000 for four-bedroom units. Households with incomes as low as $10,000/year can qualify to purchase these units.

HANDS also works to make housing development and home ownership more affordable by keeping interest rates affordable. It attempts to do this by encouraging lenders to participate in the Russell housing market. The attractiveness of such investment will be enhanced, it is believed, by the in-migration of middle-class African-American households to the area. Toward this end, HANDS sponsors a housing fair designed to present the neighborhood as a place "on the rebound," featuring attractive housing and amenities (Capek and Gilderbloom 1992). In addition, HANDS entered a partnership with the Housing Partnership, Inc. (HPI). HPI brings housing developers and financial institutions together to provide affordable housing in the Russell area. In doing so, it assists financial institutions in meeting their responsibilities under the Community Reinvestment Act.

Community Design

The final category of activities undertaken by HANDS is community design. Its Community Design Team operates out of the Urban Studies Institute at the University of Louisville. The four major activities of the Community Design Team are housing design, neighborhood housing development, neighborhood master planning, and design and crime prevention.

With regard to housing design, the Community Design Team provides advice to residents and developers on code compliance, government approvals, energy efficiency, and affordable housing designs. It assists elderly and physically challenged residents to avoid premature institutionalization by making their homes barrier-free. Figure 1 shows an interior layout and elevation for a standard HANDS-designed house. The Community Design Team also encourages the efforts of neighborhood-based housing developers and contractors by helping them meet government processing requirements, assemble financing packages, and conform to ongoing procedural stipulations during the construction process.

The Community Design Team also engages in neighborhood master planning, including creating the Russell Neighborhood Development Plan, which establishes a vision for the future development of the neighborhood. The plan draws upon an analysis of resident needs and concerns, particularly

**Figure 1
Interior Layout and Elevation of a HANDS-Designed House**

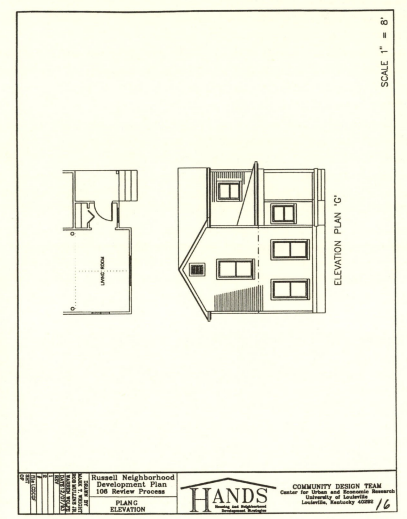

SCALE 1" = 8'

LIVING ROOM

ELEVATION PLAN 'G'

as they relate to sewers, sidewalk and street repairs, reuse or demolition of vacant buildings, recreational facilities, and increased commercial development. The plan calls for special attention to single-family housing, green space, passive recreation, and commercial and service development. It seeks to integrate middle- and low-income households, using housing that is both affordable and attractive. It also proposes to coordinate efforts with the Louisville Design Center to create a park in the old Western Cemetery, in the heart of Russell. Additionally, the plan calls for the development of compatible retail and service businesses, reinforcing HANDS's strategy to offer business start-up assistance to Russell entrepreneurs through the University of Louisville's MBA program.

The Russell Neighborhood Development Plan is an outgrowth of a joint effort by the Community Design Team and the Louisville Central Development Corporation (LCDC), a nonprofit corporation with a mission of addressing a broad range of housing, economic development, and social service issues. LCDC was required to have a neighborhood development plan in order to seek "approved developer designation" in a ten-block portion of the Russell Urban Renewal Area. The Russell Advisory Committee was so impressed by the plan LCDC and the Community Design Team generated that they requested a plan for the entire neighborhood.

Finally, the Community Design Team provides training and technical assistance on the ways in which design can be employed to prevent or mitigate crime. This is done in partnership with the University of Louisville National Crime Prevention Institute.

A very useful aspect of the HANDS effort, and one that, regrettably, is uncommon among public–private partnerships for urban redevelopment, is its evaluation component. This consists of several parts: assessment of neighborhood baseline data, tracking of participants, evaluation of training effectiveness, and the establishment of advisory committees for program monitoring.

Perspectives on HANDS

HANDS is a fascinating and imaginative project. It is unique in its comprehensive approach to neighborhood revitalization and in its structure, which includes a major university as an active partner. Comprehensive interventions focused on clients and citizens are necessary to significantly affect the complex and interrelated problems faced by disadvantaged persons and communities. Attempts to improve only housing, or infrastructure, or schools, or to provide only social services, or to offer only tax incentives do not have the power to turn a declining neighborhood around. The manner in which the HANDS project pivots on a case management system that refers clients to such diverse social, economic, and physical services as esteem training, a micro-loan program and housing is truly unusual. The visible effects of HANDS on the Russell neighborhood are already impressive.

A typical question asked about a project like HANDS is whether it tries to do too much. Could limited time and resources be better focused? This is a valid question because neither the $1.5 million in funding nor the three-year term of the project is large relative to the problems being addressed. Whether the project is spread too thin depends upon how it was conceived and is perceived. Whether stated or unstated, HANDS has at least three principal goals: (1) to build institutions and systems in Louisville that will produce results for many years to come; (2) to test intervention models and strategies; (3) to have a direct and immediate effect on the quality of life of the residents of the Russell neighborhood. These goals may sometimes be in conflict. An understanding of the value of this partnership might be achieved by viewing HANDS from each of the three perspectives defined by these goals.

As Institution Builder and Partnership Creator

An institution-building project's primary goal is to strengthen organizations and linkages so that a set of desirable activities continues long after the original funding ceases. An institution-building strategy calls for maximum utilization of existing service deliverers and focuses on promoting coordination among existing community nongovernmental organizations (NGOs) and governmental agencies. An institution-building strategy bestows credit for accomplishments upon those permanent community institutions rather than on the project.

In part because of the imaginative, comprehensive design of the program and partly because of the personalities and skills of key actors, institution-building has been a great success of HANDS. As a result of project activities and actors, city, state, and federal agencies are working together better than before. The benefits of institution-building have gone beyond the boundaries of the Russell neighborhood.

Building the partnership between the university and the community is also a major accomplishment of HANDS, which can be held out as an example for other universities. Yet, because of the vicissitudes of university politics and the difficulties associated with faculty evaluation and reward systems, establishing a university–community partnership cannot be accomplished within the three-year time frame of the project. It will take a series of successful projects over more than a decade to change the university's culture.

As Experiment

Another perspective on a short-term federally funded project of this kind is that it is a test of an innovative intervention system. To call it an experiment often elicits negative connotations of a populace being used as laboratory mice. Yet the evaluative perspective does not require that a control group exercise be conducted or that assistance to neighborhood residents be less sensitive or humane. Rather, it recognizes that by attempting to implement a comprehensive intervention system, and by documenting results, we can learn a great deal.

This experimental perspective should be part of all federally funded projects. Our nation needs to break its propensity for reinventing old solutions and repeating past mistakes. The only way to accomplish this is to learn which intervention strategies work under which circumstances, and to make this knowledge widely available. In this way, future projects in Louisville, Kentucky, and elsewhere, can begin with a better understanding of what must be done. Viewed as an experiment, the HANDS project is not spread too thin. The comprehensive nature of the project is important for the test.

As Immediate Impact

A reality of any project of this kind is that it must show tangible results during the project period. In part, this is due to political considerations external to the project. Visible achievements also ensure internal project momentum, establish client trust, and build local credibility. Hypothetically, if the HANDS project's only goal were to have the greatest positive impact on the neighborhood within the three-year funding period with the allotted $1.5 million, then the project's strategy should have been to seek out and focus upon activities that produce maximum short-term benefits. Using this hypothetical yardstick, HANDS appears to be spread too thin.

An attractive feature of the HANDS project design is the client-focused scenario that intertwines social, physical, and economic development. According to this design, the case management system comprehensively addresses the social needs of a family, moves family members toward stable employment, and ultimately toward home ownership. While this scenario is beautifully incorporated into the project design, it is complicated and difficult to accomplish in reality. For a troubled family in a troubled neighborhood, such a scenario might take a decade to play out.

If viewed simply as a three-year, direct intervention project, HANDS appears bifurcated. The education and social services side of the project functions well, as do the housing and Community Design Team side; but since three years is not sufficient time to carry many clients from the beginning of the service scenario to the end, little client, staff, or psychological connection seems to exist between these two parts of the project.

The two aspects of the project may be moving in different directions in another way. Even though few houses have been built, the home ownership program shows signs of achieving great success. A system is unfolding that combines free land, quality, low-cost design and construction, lot preparation, neighborhood design, and HUD subsidies to provide quality homes at an affordable price. An exciting outgrowth of this effort is that people who left the neighborhood but are still connected with local churches may now be willing to return and purchase a house. While this is encouraging, it may mean that existing residents, suffering severe social problems, are less likely to become home owners in the short run.

CONCLUSION

The Russell neighborhood near central Louisville, Kentucky, has experienced decades of urban decline. In a fashion typical of many declining communities, negative externalities began to magnify one another until the community lacked the perception of stability necessary to attract private investment and a vital mix of population. The housing stock deteriorated, the infrastructure aged, and the citizenry became increasingly isolated and dependent, and plagued by social disorganization. In this environment market mechanisms no longer work. The local population with the capacity to invest in the community's improvement flees the area, and outside investors do not perceive that they can receive an appropriate reward for the risk involved.

In order to reverse a downward spiral of decline and restore a situation where market forces will promote the natural process of urban renewal, someone must intervene. Because of the complex and interwoven nature of inner city neighborhood problems as exhibited in Russell, this intervention requires a comprehensive, multifaceted approach to neighborhood development.

To accomplish this multifaceted task requires a complex partnership involving a very large number of organizations, agencies, and institutions from all points on the public vs. private spectrum. These include governmental agencies, quasigovernmental authorities, for-profit and nonprofit corporations, volunteer organizations, and community associations, each contributing to the endeavor what it does best.

HANDS is a unique project that offers a fascinating and challenging comprehensive approach to neighborhood revitalization. Perhaps its greatest strength lies in the multiple-level institutional partnerships, involving both public and private participants, that it has created and strengthened. Of particular note are the university–community partnership that has been launched, and the special role a university can play in leading the complex partnership structure necessary for this kind of project.

Because HANDS views public–private partnerships as a process rather than just an agreement between organizations, it has established partnerships with the potential to survive and thrive many years into the future. Furthermore, its design, which attempts to address the social and economic aspects of redevelopment as well as the physical, takes into account equity issues that other redevelopment efforts have been criticized for ignoring (Krumholz 1984; Thomas 1984).

Because of the special assets of the Russell neighborhood and because of the special effort made by the partnership described above, Russell shows signs of reversing negative trends and developing positive momentum. It appears that, at this point, what HANDS needs most is additional time and funding to fully develop its structure, its institutional partnerships, and its momentum toward positively affecting the lives of the Russell neighborhood's residents.

CHAPTER 6

Incubation: Breaking Out

PUBLIC–PRIVATE PARTNERSHIPS FOR SMALL BUSINESS DEVELOPMENT

The goals and objectives of urban redevelopment efforts vary from one context to the next, as do the strategies employed to accomplish them. One approach to redevelopment focuses on the creation of small, indigenous firms as a means to locally sustainable job creation and income generation. Small business creation has the advantage of perfecting markets by increasing the number of independent buyers and sellers of goods and services while promoting innovative new products.

This chapter begins with an examination of the nature of small businesses and their role in a free market economy. It then defines and discusses small business incubation as an enterprise development tool. The chapter concludes with three case studies. The first is the Arizona Technology Incubator, located in Scottsdale, as an example of a successful incubator created by a public–private partnership. The second is small business development in southwestern Michigan utilizing a BIDCO and a special industrial park. The third case views the Hungarian nation's difficult transition from a Communist to a free market economy. It addresses the role of small business incubation in that transition and looks at the activities of the Local Enterprise Agencies there.

THE ROLE OF SMALL BUSINESS IN THE ECONOMY

Defining "Small Business"

While there seems to be a consensus that small businesses are essential to a free market economic system, that consensus breaks down when defining the term *small business*. Some have argued that this definitional disagreement makes it difficult to make an accurate assessment of the economic contributions of these entities (Peterson et al. 1986; Spencer-Hull 1986; Blackford 1991). As recently as 1988, the U.S. Small Business Administration (SBA) admitted that a standard definition of "small business" was nonexistent (Blackford 1991).

Multiple definitions of *small business* are in currency. One views a small business as one that has a name, a place of operation, an owner, and one or more employees. Another defines a small business as one that is managed by three or fewer individuals, or that has 100 or fewer employees. Businesses that employ 500 or fewer workers also have been labeled "small." Still another definition views a business as small when it is independently owned and operated and employs 100 or fewer, or has gross receipts of less than $1 million (Peterson et al. 1986; Spencer-Hull 1986). Definitions that contain dollar amounts are difficult to use for international comparisons.

A widely accepted definition of *small business* comes from the SBA. Section 3 of the Small Business Act of 1953 classifies any business that is independently owned and operated and not dominant in its field as "small" (Peterson et al. 1986; Spencer-Hull 1986; Blackford 1991). Despite this, the SBA has continued to use many varied definitions, depending on industrial classification. For example, during the late 1950s, any industrial establishment employing fewer than 250 people was considered "small." On the other hand, a "small" wholesaler was one with annual sales equal to, or less than, $5 million. Retail and service businesses could qualify as "small" if they had yearly sales of $1 million or less (Blackford 1991).

In 1988, the SBA proposed a uniform classification of businesses by number of employees, across industries. Under this system, a firm with fewer than 20 employees is designated as "very small"; one with 20 to 99 employees is "small"; 100 to 499 employees constitutes a "medium-sized" firm; and a business with 500 or more employees is considered "large" (Blackford 1991). This classification system is extensively used today.

A Brief History of Small Business

In his classic book *The Wealth of Nations*, published in 1776, Adam Smith referred to an economy dominated by small businesses. In fact, it is reasonably safe to assume that virtually all establishments in Smith's economy were "small" (Solomon 1986). The small firm might be viewed as the original manifestation of modern capitalism. During the Middle Ages, the small businesses established by traders and runaway serfs to serve the nobility ultimately shifted the balance of power from the latter to the former and provided the foundation upon which the economies of most of today's world rest (Solomon 1986).

In the United States, at about the time that *The Wealth of Nations* first appeared, small businesses came into evidence. Typically, they were run by artisans and tradesmen, such as cobblers, tailors, silversmiths, blacksmiths, and hatmakers. In rural communities, the general store was the predominant form of small business. It often served as a retail outlet, a mail depot, and a credit source all in one (Solomon 1986; Blackford 1991).

Some thriving American small businessmen began to import industrial technologies from Great Britain. This resulted in the early light manufacturing industry. As U.S. businesses successfully lured foreign investment, these firms and the economy began to grow dramatically (Solomon 1986; Blackford 1991).

The distinction between "small" and "big" business became increasingly pronounced in the post–Civil War era. The U.S. economy had become national, and big business was viewed as the driving economic force. Small businesses were considered to play an ancillary role. Smith's economy of small businesses and his concept of perfect competition were forever altered (Solomon 1986). By 1914, one-third of the American labor force worked in firms having more than 500 employees (Blackford 1991).

Small businesses adapted to this changing situation in several ways. Some moved toward labor-intensive enterprises. Others pursued markets eschewed by large firms that felt they lacked competitive advantage. Still others merely closed their doors. A few competed successfully, and others innovated. The rise of the service sector is attributed to small business. Nevertheless, the balance of opportunities has tended to favor big business (Solomon 1986; Blackford 1991).

With recent transformations in the global economic structure, most mature industrial economies are experiencing fundamental changes. The global structure is shifting from an insular national economy to an interdependent global economy (Solomon 1986; Spencer-Hull 1986). Some have called this a new industrial revolution. In this revolution, the U.S. economic system is in competition with those of Japan, Europe, and the emerging industrial nations of Asia (e.g.; Taiwan, Singapore, and South Korea). Eastern European countries, with antiquated equipment and business practices, must compete with the West.

No longer can any society rely on past achievements to ensure future success (Solomon 1986; Burrus 1993). The emphasis is now on innovation, particularly in knowledge-intensive industries, such as computers, biotechnology, and telecommunications. Entrepreneurship and ingenuity are in demand as never before. The economic game is being played under a new set of rules that must be understood and accepted if success is to be achieved (Solomon 1986; Burrus 1993).

In this new era of transformation, small businesses are seen by some to be a hidden asset (Solomon 1986; Spencer-Hull 1986). They argue that small firms act as a catalyst in the transition from the "smokestack" economy to the global economy (Solomon 1986), or the engine that will drive redevelopment (Spencer-Hull 1986). Entrepreneurship has become the new hope. Thus, while small business has always played an important role in the "American dream," it has enjoyed perhaps unprecedented attention since the mid-1970s (Solomon 1986; Blackford 1991).

How Small Business Is Important to the Economy

Small businesses have made major contributions to the U.S. economy in recent years in the areas of employment, innovation, and economic diversity. Relative to employment, firms with fewer than 500 workers employ roughly half of the U.S. workforce. Jobs created by such firms account for two-thirds of the total (Bendick and Egan 1991).

In 1990, the nation experienced its first economic downturn in eight years. While small firms were certainly affected (new incorporations declined), they continued to create new jobs even as large corporations were laying employees off (U.S. Small Business Administration 1991).

Small businesses play an important role in product innovation in all societies. Some argue that less expensive and more original innovations emanate from small firms. Large firms are typically the source of innovations that involve higher development costs and less deviation from traditional and established principles (Rothwell and Zegveld 1982; Campbell 1988). Some regional development studies have shown that when technology-based corporations collaborate with innovative new firms, the result is a greater potential for long-term growth in employment (Oakey 1984).

Most small businesses find it prohibitively expensive to carry out the time-consuming basic research necessary for innovation and large-scale commercialization (Rothwell and Zegveld 1982; Solomon 1986). Thus, an interaction between large and small firms is necessary to bring product innovations to market (Rothwell and Zegveld 1982). This has, in part, given rise to the practice termed *intrapreneuring* (Pinchot 1986).

By virtue of its diversity, the small business sector of the economy helps to diversify the greater national economy. Small businesses represent a rich and varied network of suppliers, subcontractors, and distributors that work in a complementary fashion with large corporations, augmenting the efficiency, flexibility, and balance of the overall economy (Solomon 1986). They perfect markets by adding to the number of buyers and sellers of products and raw materials. In accordance with the ecological principle known as Ashby's Law, the increased economic diversity afforded by small businesses yields stability in the economic system (see Baldwin 1985, p. 10).

The Problems Facing Small Businesses

While small businesses are relatively easy to start, they are difficult to sustain. In their first three to five years of operation, most small businesses must make several difficult transitions from fledgling enterprise to stable firm. The need for infusions of capital is greatest during this period. One need only examine the statistics on business failures in the United States to begin to understand how difficult it is to take a new enterprise to maturity. Estimates of the percentage of new start-ups that fail within the first three to five years range anywhere from 40 percent to 90 percent Buccino (1989) found that 10 percent failed in the first year.

Explanations for this high rate of failure are many, but four stand out: (1) poor management; (2) undercapitalization; (3) relatively high overhead costs (compared with larger firms); and (4) a lack of savvy in selecting, defining, and pursuing a market (Vesper 1983; Solomon 1986; Campbell 1988; Lyons 1990). Inexperienced management is the chief cause of small business failure. Entrepreneurs are typically people with good ideas or a high degree of skill or knowledge in their particular field. They are not necessarily competent business managers (Campbell 1988), and they often lack the ability to manage an inventory or keep books (Solomon 1986; Campbell 1988). Such deficiencies can easily destroy even a well-capitalized business.

While lack of financial capital afflicts most businesses, small firms are particularly affected (Solomon 1986; Chemical Bank 1984). This circumstance often precludes the purchase of state-of-the-art equipment and shortens investment time horizons. These problems may lower profits, reduce rates of retained earnings, and stifle reinvestment. All of them serve to keep the business small and, ultimately, not viable (Solomon 1986).

Due to the economies of scale in purchasing supplies, services, space, and so on, the per unit cost of doing business is lower for large companies than for small. This makes it more difficult for small firms to finance their operations over time.

Lack of savvy in selecting a market results in many small firms putting themselves in direct competition with larger, more efficient ones. It may also result in entry into a field that is rapidly dwindling due to obsolescence (Solomon 1986; Campbell 1988). Not defining one's product and delineating one's market clearly may result in a shotgun approach to marketing and product development that drains resources without producing results.

The Business Incubation Solution

The case has been made for the value of small business to a local economy. The preceding discussion also makes it apparent that economic development strategies focused on small firms are fraught with risk. To have a chance of success, these strategies must do more than merely encourage entrepreneurship and new enterprise creation. They must nurture young firms to maturity.

One local economic development tool that aims both to create new firms and to foster their growth is small business incubation. Lichtenstein and Lyons (1996) have defined *business incubation* as "programs that assist in the formation, development and survival of new enterprises." Incubation is a rapidly growing technique used for enterprise development, with a new program opening its doors at a rate of approximately one per week in the United States, Canada, and Mexico (NBIA 1995). These programs manifest themselves in a variety of ways, but the most common is the *small business incubator.*

Typically, an incubator has been a building, such as a former factory or warehouse, that has been retrofitted for its new purpose. A growing number of incubators in North America are now purpose-built. The building is subdivided into small, varied spaces that are useful for a variety of start-up firms. Incubators commonly use movable walls to allow tenant businesses to expand their operations when they are ready to do so. Incubators may house anywhere from one to over 100 tenants at a time, depending on size, location, and mission.

According to Allen and Rahman (1985, p. 12) "incubators provide the assistance that fills the knowledge gaps, reduces early stage operational costs such as rent and service fees and establishes entrepreneurs in a local enterprise support network." In essence, incubators strive to mitigate the problems, described above, that cause young businesses to fail.

Lichtenstein and Lyons (1996) characterize the role of business incubators in a somewhat different way. They point out that entrepreneurs require certain resources if their businesses are to succeed. These resources can be classified into four major types: (1) a business concept (an innovative and marketable product or service idea); (2) physical resources (e.g., space, raw materials, capital, etc.); (3) core competencies/skills (e.g., technical, management, financial, etc.); and (4) market (e.g., customers, distribution channels, transportation, etc.).

Lichtenstein and Lyons (1996) further specify that entrepreneurs face obstacles to obtaining these resources. They have identified nine types of barriers to successful entrepreneurship: lack of availability, lack of awareness, lack of affordability, transaction barriers, lack of self-awareness, lack of personal accountability, emotions, lack of capability, and lack of creativity. The role of the incubator is to develop and adopt specific practices (services, activities, programs, etc.) that assist their client entrepreneurs in overcoming these obstacles (Lichtenstein and Lyons 1996).

The most common incubation practices employed to mitigate the obstacles described above include providing space at below market rents; providing shared services, such as photocopying, clerical assistance, reception, and use of a conference room; offering management assistance, including seminars, mentoring programs, and business plan development counseling; assisting with financing (e.g., operating revolving loan funds and interceding with local lending institutions); and providing the opportunity to network with other tenant firms and with businesses in the greater community (Campbell 1988; Lyons 1990). As the business incubation movement grows and matures, its practices become increasingly numerous and sophisticated (Lichtenstein and Lyons 1996; Rice and Matthews 1995; Tornatzky et al. 1996).

Business incubation in its present form is relatively new to North America. The concept originated in Europe and did not arrive on this side of the Atlantic until the late 1970s (Campbell 1988). The National Business Incubation Association reports that approximately fifty business incubators operated in North America in 1984 (NBIA 1990). By the end of 1994, nearly

500 served almost 7,800 client entrepreneurs (NBIA 1995). This represents a tenfold growth over ten years.

Incubation programs in the United States first developed for any one of three distinct reasons. Some started as a mechanism for redeveloping blighted inner city neighborhoods. Present day "empowerment incubator" programs continue this tradition. Other incubators were initiated by the National Science Foundation (NSF) as part of an experiment in entrepreneurship fostered through certain institutions of higher education. The many university-based, high-technology incubation programs found throughout the country succeed these NSF-sponsored efforts. Finally, successful entrepreneurs and investor groups founded several early incubators, a practice that continues today (Campbell 1988).

Current sponsorship of incubation programs reflects these historical roots. Local governments focusing on community and economic development sponsor many incubation programs. University sponsors, seeking more rapid research and technology transfer, have grown in number in recent years, and privately sponsored incubators continue to make up a portion of the total.

Incubator researchers have classified program sponsors into five major categories: public agencies, nonprofit organizations, universities, private corporations, and public–private partnerships (Allen and Rahman 1985; Lyons 1990). The last sponsorship category is the fastest growing. Increasingly small business incubators are sponsored by partnerships of public and private entities. This is a departure from the early incubators, which were either distinctly public, with a focus on job creation, or explicitly private, with a revenue generation concentration. This suggests that both sectors have come to realize the mutual redevelopment benefits to be obtained through a collaborative approach to enterprise development.

Following is a description and discussion of one of the best-known examples of an incubation program sponsored by a public–private partnership, the Arizona Technology Incubator.

THE ARIZONA TECHNOLOGY INCUBATOR

The Arizona Technology Incubator (ATI) emerged from the collaborative thinking of Arizona State University President Lattie Coor and Alan Hald, vice chairman of MicroAge and then president of the Arizona Innovation Network. They envisioned strengthening the Arizona economy through a public–private partnership involving the university, various governmental agencies, and private entities. The purpose would be to share resources and assist technology-based businesses.

Technology-based firms were selected as the beneficiaries of this assistance because of their rate of success relative to other businesses. Various studies have found that high-technology firms have the lowest failure rate among new enterprises (Cooper 1982; Campbell 1988). Furthermore, it was reasoned, successful technology firms channel their innovations back into the system, benefiting other businesses.

The Partnership

The roster of major partners in this economic development effort includes private corporations, utilities, venture capital firms, municipalities, quasipublic economic development organizations, state government agencies, and institutions of higher education. These are shown in Figure 2. Specific organizations include the following:

- Arizona Innovation Network
- Arizona Public Service Company
- Arizona State University
- City of Scottsdale
- Columbine Venture Funds
- Fairchild Data Corporation
- Greater Phoenix Economic Council
- Salt River Project
- Scottsdale Industrial Development Authority
- Snell and Wilmer
- State of Arizona Department of Commerce
- US West

In addition, donations of money, time, services, and equipment have been made by Greyhound Financial, Intel, Lewis & Roca, MicroAge, Motorola, Northern Trust Bank of Arizona, O'Connor Cavanagh, Phoenix Newspapers, and Streich Lang, as well as numerous other companies and individuals.

This partnership is more informal than formal in nature. Since its inception, ATI itself has played the leadership role in maintaining, directing, and expanding the partnership. ATI is currently pursuing an ambitious effort aimed at adding new partners, with an emphasis on banks and additional

Figure 2
The ATI Partnership

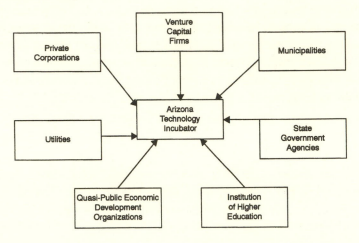

high-tech firms. The incubation program has retained a professional fund-raising consultant to assist in this effort. This latter undertaking has the full support of all the ATI partners, as it will help spread the financial and time burdens involved.

ATI

The Arizona Technology Incubator is the tangible manifestation of this partnership arrangement. It is a 23,000-square-foot facility located in the Scottsdale Commerce Center, a business office park in suburban Phoenix. The facility is modern and situated on one level. It includes office and laboratory space, meeting rooms, common areas, and a lunch and break area with kitchen.

ATI's mission statement spells out its overall goal, defining the program as a specialized incubator with a focus on technology-related businesses. Its mission is "to increase the survival odds of promising, technology based firms by providing business services, marketing and management support." To carry out this mission, ATI has adopted practices aimed at identifying appropriate clients and meeting their needs, as well as insuring the viability of the incubation program. These practices include a selective entry policy; a combination residential/affiliates program; a carefully selected package of business services and other assistance; a clear graduation policy; a three-tiered executive board structure; and an aggressive program for financing the incubator. Each of these is discussed in more detail below.

Many business incubation programs have entry policies, requirements that prospective clients must meet in order to qualify for access to the program. These policies vary with the nature and mission of the incubation program in question. In keeping with its mission, ATI admits only "promising technology based firms." Clients are selected on the basis of their growth potential, product proprietary position, marketability, financing needs, and company structure. ATI's position is that a company that fails is more harmful to the economy than one that never began operations. Thus, only entrepreneurs perceived to have a good chance of surviving the rigors of enterprise development in the highly competitive technology markets are offered support.

This policy appears harsh on its surface, but the purpose of an incubator is not to aid fledgling businesses that would not survive if left unprotected. To understand ATI's position, two important factors must be considered. First, an incubation program is itself a business. Successful incubation programs are operated as such, with a focus on becoming self-sustaining. If the incubation program fails, support for its client firms abruptly ceases. This is equally true for public-serving incubators and private, profit-driven programs. Spending incubator resources on businesses with little or no chance of success jeopardizes the incubator's financial position, and ultimately its survival. Incubation program managers often say that one of their most important roles is to "tell people when they have no business being in business." Second, high-technology businesses are unique in the level of resources they require and the degree of competition they face. A technology-based incubator must manage its resources wisely if it is to succeed.

A second practice utilized by ATI is a combined residential/affiliates incubation program. Most business incubators are so-called residential programs. That is, the client firms are housed exclusively in the incubator facility. This structure offers several advantages, among them control over the factors in the environment of the fledgling business and a situation that is conducive to interfirm networking. However, it also limits the number of entrepreneurs who can be served and could act to isolate the incubator and its clients from the larger community of which they are a part. Many incubation programs now operate both residential facilities and affiliates programs. The latter is an incubator without walls. It makes most of the same services provided to its tenants available to entrepreneurs in the community. Affiliates pay a monthly fee. By adopting this arrangement, ATI has both avoided the limitations of a residential incubator and generated a new source of income for its operations. Recently, ATI expanded the affiliates program by entering into negotiations with a firm that would physically remain in California but become an affiliate of the program. At present, ATI serves twenty client firms: fourteen tenants (which its management calls "associates") and six affiliates. Two affiliates have graduated from the residential program and choose to retain access to the incubator's network of experts.

All true business incubation programs provide a package of "shared services" to their clients. ATI is no exception. It offers certain services for a fee, and others at no charge to its client entrepreneurs. Among those services available for a fee are secretarial, photocopying, faxing, accounting, market research, press releases, word processing, telephone answering, newsletter publishing, and bookkeeping. Free services include use of furniture, conference rooms, kitchen facilities, receptionist services, and a notary. The fact that these services are shared, and that some of them are donated, helps keep their cost below market.

Another practice adopted by ATI in pursuing its mission is enforcement of a strict graduation policy. Generally, incubator tenants that leave the facility stronger than when they entered are known as "graduates." The way in which the decision is made as to when to "graduate" a tenant varies widely among incubators. Often publicly sponsored incubators set an arbitrary deadline by which a given tenant must move on (e.g., two years or three years). This approach evolved from pressure to serve as many entrepreneurs as possible, and sometimes results in "kicking fledglings out of the nest before they can fly." Privately sponsored incubators, on the other hand, tend to allow tenants to stay indefinitely, so as to ensure uninterrupted cash flow to the incubator. This greatly limits the number of entrepreneurs served, and causes the incubator to behave more like an office or industrial park.

Due to its public–private support, ATI is not overly influenced by either of these pressures. Instead, it handles graduation situations case by case, discussing this with each firm upon entry. ATI requires that prior to graduation, a company must have established the following: market presence, a functional sales plan, administrative procedures, adequate financing, and a management team. Thus, tenants do move on, but not until they are deemed ready. Axtell Development Corporation was the first firm to graduate from ATI, in November 1994. It continues its association with the incubation program, as an affiliate.

Most business incubation experts list a strong, competent board of directors among the elements crucial to incubator program success. ATI has taken full advantage of its partnership underpinnings to create a three-tiered board structure. The six-member Executive Board, which meets monthly, is the uppermost tier. This group oversees the basic operations of ATI. The second tier is the Full Board. This group has fourteen members, and meets with the Executive Board once per quarter. The third tier of ATI's board structure is the nine-member Advisory Board. This latter group meets quarterly to make recommendations to the incubation program. Board membership is by invitation only. Most members have served since ATI's inception.

In addition, the ATI board structure has a relatively elaborate committee system, consisting of five major committees: the Executive Committee, Finance Committee, Facilities & Administration Committee, Communications & Public Relations Committee, and Strategic Planning Subcommittee of the Executive Committee. The Executive Committee does double duty as the Board Development & Nominating Committee. The Finance Committee is responsible for budgeting and auditing, and oversees fund-raising activities. It also assists clients in financial matters related to their businesses. The Facilities & Administration Committee carries out the incubator's admissions policy, manages the facilities, and handles staffing, compensation of incubation program staff, and evaluation of staff performance. As its name implies, the Communications & Public Relations Committee handles internal and external communications and public relations. The Strategic Planning Subcommittee is responsible for developing ATI's three-year strategic plan and coordinating the Advisory Board's participation in that activity. It has principal responsibility for ensuring that the public–private partnership survives and thrives.

The final major practice that ATI utilizes to achieve its mission is its method of financing its operations. It actually employs a range of financing methods: Arizona State University, governmental agencies, and private enterprises have all acted as sources of revenue. In addition, the incubation program relies on income from rent and other payments made by client firms. Grants, donations, and client fees are traditional incubator financing mechanisms, but ATI also generates revenues by a less commonly employed means: through returns on equity shares and royalties from both tenant and affiliate firms. In this way, ATI has literally invested in the success of its clients.

How Has ATI Benefited Its Partners and Its Community?

A successful incubation program like ATI can yield a win–win situation for all those involved (both directly and indirectly). Client entrepreneurs win in that they gain the support necessary for successful enterprise development. The commercialization of research and the educational and business opportunities afforded by the process serve to benefit the university partners, their faculties, staff, and students. State and local government partners win through job creation, an expanded tax base, and, ultimately, a diversified economy. Private investors in the partnership benefit through commercial and industrial real estate development. They also profit by investing in the incubator's client firms. In addition to the monetary profit made by private partners, involvement with the business incubation program provides a good opportunity to enhance their public image. Finally, existing businesses in the community (outside the incubation program) derive benefit from the development of new technologies and increased investment and marketing opportunities.

ATI has conducted an economic impact analysis of its operations for 1994. It also has projected its impact for 1999. Direct impacts in 1994 included the following:

- 68 jobs created
- $2,126,000 in total wages and salaries
- $3,463,000 in total annual sales
- $163,459 total tax revenues generated.

Indirect benefits for 1994 included the creation of thirty-two additional jobs. These are multiplier-effect jobs generated by businesses that serve incubation program clients in some way. ATI projects that by 1999, it will have contributed the following direct benefits to its community:

- 2,010 jobs created
- $59,581,800 in total wages and salaries
- $131,500,000 in total annual sales
- $4,270,500 in total taxes.

Projected indirect benefits by 1999 include the creation of 858 additional jobs.

An added intangible benefit to the state and local economies emanates from the efforts of ATI. All of the incubator's twenty client firms are in the manufacturing/engineering-related sector. This sector is highly important, particularly in comparison with the growing service sector. If one subscribes to economic base theory, it is understood that the growth of the manufacturing sector is the key to a strong economy. Manufacturing firms form an essential primary job component of the economy.

Thus, it can be said that the Arizona Technology Incubator yields tangible and intangible benefits to each of its partners and to the larger community (local, state, and, arguably, national) as well. By the yardstick of "mutual benefit," it is an example of a successful public–private partnership. Measured against its mission, it would appear to be a successful incubation program as well. While ATI focuses its efforts on only a small economic development niche, leaving itself vulnerable to criticism that it is not an equitable development mechanism, one should note that it is but one tool in its state's, and its local community's, economic development strategy. It cannot realistically be expected to solve all of the community's development problems. Other tools must be implemented to address the remaining issues.

AN INDUSTRIAL PARK IN SOUTHWESTERN MICHIGAN

In southwestern Michigan an unusual industrial park is evolving that is the product of a unique private–public partnership process. In the previous sentence the words "public" and "private" are reversed from their typical order because the entire process has been initiated from the private side. As society begins to understand that public purpose and private profit can be pursued through collaborative processes, and as business leaders feel greater comfort working with mixed economic systems, the partnership process will be increasingly initiated by the private sector (Sandstedt 1995).

A private landowner in a southwestern Michigan community owns a large parcel of property, next to the municipal airport, that surrounds his small industrial operation. He wishes to create an industrial park with his land. In pursuit of his goal, the landowner contacted Capitol BIDCO, Inc., of Lansing, MI. Capitol BIDCO is a for-profit corporation with a public purpose that is licensed by the state of Michigan.

The BIDCO

The Business Industrial Development Corporation (BIDCO) law was enacted to promote small business and industry. BIDCOs do this by making business loans and providing technical assistance. The loans they provide might be described as medium risk/reward loans. They are too risky for banks but not appropriate for venture capital. The recipient of the loan is typically a small, established firm that needs to expand because of new product lines or business growth opportunities. This kind of debt capital is imperative for small business development because most small firms ready to expand find it difficult to obtain financing elsewhere. If medium-risk capital is not available in a community, businesses are stifled at a critical time in their life cycle (see "BIDCO Financing" in Chapter 4). It is like cutting all protein and calcium out of the diet of all of the town's three-year-old children.

As a nonbank lender, Capitol BIDCO received all of its liquidity from equity investments rather than deposits from the public. As a result, it comes under a set of regulations different from banks that allow it to pursue a higher risk/reward loan market (Williams 1986). Capitol BIDCO's typical loan is at 12 percent, fully amortized in five years, and subordinated to a bank loan (see "Second Position Loans," Chapter 4). The BIDCO also requires an equity kicker in the form of royalties or warrants (see "Equality Injections and Equity Kickers," Chapter 4). Like ATI, the equity kicker keeps Capitol BIDCO emotionally and financially invested in the success of each client company. Capitol BIDCO typically has the right to a seat on the board of directors of its clients but generally prefers a nonvoting advisory presence (Sandstedt 1995).

The equity investors who have provided the base funding for Capitol BIDCO represent the entire spectrum of organizational types from public to private. They include a municipally owned power and light utility, two commercial banks, a health maintenance organization, a municipal employee pension fund, an investment partnership, a private venture capital firm, and a regional growth alliance. A growth alliance is a nonprofit county or multicounty economic development organization with funding from the state, the city, the county, and several private firms. The project that is the focus of this case study is not in the jurisdiction of any of the governmental entities that have invested in the BIDCO: they come from all parts of the state.

The BIDCO's stock is divided into two classes (see "Multiple Classes of Common Stock," Chapter 4). Once the various investors purchased their stock, the state government matched this investment with one dollar of government stock purchases for every $2.50 of other equity. The equity owned by the state is in a different class than that purchased by the other public and private investors. This special class of stock has three covenants enumerated in the articles of incorporation: (1) the stock is nonvoting, (2) the stock is subordinated to the other class, and (3) during the period when the state owns shares, the BIDCO can work only with small businesses in that state. The BIDCO has the right to buy out the state ownership at any time (Sandstedt 1995).

The special way in which the state injects equity into the BIDCO accomplishes several things. First, as equity, it provides an investment that strengthens the BIDCO's balance sheet and makes it easier for the BIDCO to attract private debt capital. Second, the subordinated nature of the stock makes it less difficult to attract other private equity. Third, the "in state" covenant ensures that the taxpayers of the state receive the immediate benefit from this mixed sector enterprise.

Unlike most banks, for a fee BIDCOs are allowed to provide clients with consulting services related to their loans. In the case of this southwestern Michigan site, Steven L. Sandstedt, vice president of Capital BIDCO is managing the process of land use planning, zoning, and site design services for the industrial park. When the park is sufficiently under way, Capitol BIDCO will coordinate property management services as well (Sandstedt 1995).

Capitol BIDCO also has formed a subsidiary venture capital firm with SBIC certification that may invest in firms entering the park. SBIC (Small Business Investment Company) is a very old public–private partnership program initiated by the U.S. government in the 1950s. It lends federal money to a certified venture capital firm in a ratio to the amount of private investment raised, providing the federal money and the matching private investment are used for venture capital investment.

The Industrial Park

The plans for the park are unique for the region. The industrial lots are organized as a condominium with streets and utilities owned in common. This gives the developer and the businesses entering the park control over their own infrastructure through their condominium association. Infrastructure will be managed and maintained by the BIDCO under contract with the condominium association (see "Mixed Condominiums," Chapter 4). The zoning falls under the local planned unit development ordinance.

Sometimes real estate losses resulting from depreciation write-offs can provide tax benefits to the owners of a business coming into the park. This condominium arrangement gives them the option of purchasing the space for their industry to facilitate using those tax advantages. They may buy their facilities through an SBA certified development company loan with a very small down payment and/or receive a loan from the BIDCO. In some cases personal tax advantages result if the business owners buy real estate personally or through a partnership, then lease the space to their industrial corporation. The certified development corporation program allows this through an "alter ego" provision. If they do not want to buy, they may rent space in the industrial park from the condominium developer.

An additional advantage of the condominium arrangement is that as firms grow, lot lines can be changed without going through subdivision ordinance control each time. The lot change requires only an amendment to the condominium master deed. This also allows for a condominium within a condominium. An industrial building planned on one of the sites will be divided with movable walls. This arrangement provides very small businesses with a flexible place in which to get started. Because it is a condominium building within the industrial park mega-condominium, small companies locating there will have the "alter ego" tax advantage mentioned above.

Common areas in the building, such as office space, meeting rooms, and a reception area, create an incubator-like structure. This space is owned in common as a part of the condominium within a condominium master deed. Renting firms have use of common space and infrastructure as a part of their lease. All firms pay for other services, which may include the types of services offered at most incubators.

The end result is an intersectoral process involving several kinds of businesses and several levels of government and quasigovernmental organizations that is initiated by private actors. Each balances its own set of risks and potential rewards with its other agendas. The product of this process is a kind of second-stage incubator, one that takes small and young, but established, companies and offers all of the ingredients for their growth and success.

The industrial park provides high-quality land and infrastructure, the BIDCO furnishes intermediate-risk investment capital, the venture capital subsidiary offers venture capital, and the BIDCO staff affords technical assistance related to small business management, marketing, and research. The equity kicker arrangement of any BIDCO loan means that this public–private entity will remain financially and emotionally invested in the industrial park and its businesses. The public policy objective of promoting the growth and success of small industries will be achieved.

HUNGARY'S LOCAL ENTERPRISE AGENCIES

The Context

Local economic development in Hungary provides a fascinating example of an economy without walls between the traditional sectors. Hungary was for decades a resistive member of the Eastern European Communist bloc. While a kind of private ownership of housing survived throughout the Communist era, the state owned nearly all commercial and industrial activities (Hegedus and Tosics 1993).

In 1991, when Hungary broke with its Communist past, the government rewrote the constitution. Perhaps as a reaction to the central authority of the Communist era, the new constitution vests highly autonomous power in local government and turns over nearly all of the Communist-owned property to local authorities. Furthermore, municipalities are given nearly complete flexibility to act as both private corporations and public bodies (Virag 1995). The law also allows great flexibility in the relationship between local units of government. They may create joint ventures among themselves to provide a public service, to operate an enterprise, or to join with a private firm.

Some argue that the national government gave power to local authorities to avoid dealing with the difficulties of property ownership and disposal, but Ministry of the Interior officials claim Hungary "created the most liberal system of local government in Europe to promote a market economy, decentralize national power, and give local decision makers a central role in promoting economic development" (Virag 1995). For whatever reason, Hungarian local governments were handed the opportunity to be on the cutting edge of the worldwide movement toward political decentralization and public–private collaboration.

Hungary lacked experience with market economics. Local officials knew little about collecting taxes because resources had always come from the state. They had poor skills in managing property, running businesses, or collaborating with the fledgling private sector. Nor did many know how to negotiate with the multinational corporations interested in Hungary's well-educated, low-cost labor force (Virag 1995).

Some communities near the Austrian border have been active in both privatization of old companies and attraction of new firms (Virag 1995). From 1992 to 1994, Western commentators considered Hungary a leader and a model of Eastern European transition to a free market economy (Woodward 1995). Yet communities in the eastern part of the country are experiencing very high unemployment, in excess of 50 percent in many cities (Levai 1995). Many of eastern Hungary's heavy industries could not compete with Western firms. The region was hardest hit by the change from supplying industries in the Eastern bloc to selling to the West. This change was more rapid than for some other Eastern European countries because "many new era politicians in Hungary burned their bridges to the East and cut off their supplier relationships to industries of the CIS" (Kiss 1995).

Also, roads are poor east of Budapest, which reduces the competitiveness of existing firms and decreases communities' ability to attract Western companies. Relations with Romania are strained by conflicts over treatment of the ethnic Hungarian population living in Transylvania, a situation that has exacerbated trade problems on the eastern border. Since social assistance is a local function, "social assistance payments to the poor are becoming a heavy burden in the old manufacturing center of the eastern part of the country" (Levai 1995).

Now voters are expressing dissatisfaction with even the privatization carried out in the western part of the country. Many say that the deals struck with foreign firms sold off the nation's business assets too cheaply. The public sees little benefit accruing to the average citizen from the privatization, for the people are witnessing the daily reduction of public and social services.

Public attitude toward the private sector in general is also a problem. Many people do not understand the concept of a private entrepreneur. Based on past experience, a feeling persists that anybody who is successful at making money must be cheating (Eder 1995). The notion that some might succeed through hard work and innovative thinking is totally foreign. Because of recent elections, government policy exhibits a new "go slow" attitude with respect to its transition to a free market economy (Woodward 1995).

The overall results of Hungary's experiment with local government autonomy since 1991 are mixed. Ninety percent of the housing stock has been privatized, but in most cases, at politically induced prices that averaged only 7 to 9 percent of market value (Hegedus 1995). Now, local communities face severe economic constraints. They have generally failed to develop new sources of tax revenues. While municipalities have a broad range of powers to tax, local officials feel that the population has no capacity to be taxed. Some Hungarian economists disagree (Hegedus 1995). Transfer payments from the state still account for 80 to 90 percent of local revenues, but the national government must now cut its allocations to localities due to the economic downturn and increasing national debt.

Most municipalities have not capitalized on their flexibility to stimulate economic development with new business ventures or partnership arrangements. One national official stated:

It is generally not considered by local leaders to be the responsibility of the local government to promote business development. This difference in understanding is a big problem. Generally speaking, in order for local governments to further economic development in Hungary, there needs to be a change in consciousness. It is essential to move toward market-oriented attitudes and structures. (Virag 1995)

As a result of revenue shortages, local governments are selling off their commercial and industrial assets to raise money for social services. With a few shining exceptions, they are disposing of urban assets without an understanding of how markets function in general, or how urban real estate markets work in particular (Virag 1995).

Despite some problems, GDP has dropped by only about 12 percent from its peak, the currency is relatively stable, and the population has a positive view of the future (Andorka 1995). Local officials are seeking training in the skills that they need in their new roles, and new small businesses are being started every day.

The Local Enterprise Assistance Program

While cities in the eastern part of the country are under severe stress, they do have some assets. One is a stable, well educated population. Since people are quite reluctant to give up their apartments, most of the previous members of the middle class are staying in their hometowns (Levai 1995). Unemployed people in the eastern region are receiving some financial assistance from the government and are in need of products and services. An educated workforce and a market for small business development are therefore present. One program that is helping the society make the transition to a free market economy without selling off its assets is the Local Enterprise Assistance Program. This program, designed to promote the development of small business in Hungary, has independent offices in several counties. A minimal staff is paid for partly by the state and partly by each participating county (To'th 1995).

The local enterprise assistance agency staff provides technical assistance to small businesses, through both workshops and one-on-one consultation. Technical assistance attempts to address all of the difficulties faced by small businesses. The agency promotes better bookkeeping skills and marketing techniques, and helps entrepreneurs define their products and delineate feasible markets for each. It also teaches personnel management and financial projection techniques, and helps the business pull everything together into a good business plan. It attempts to assist entrepreneurs in finding start-up capital and using it wisely. Some effort is also made to network with businesses within the country and promote communication with companies in Western Europe.

In short, enterprise assistance agencies are an incubation program, generally of the type labeled small business development centers in the United States. Some of the local enterprise assistance agencies have incubator buildings or work with independent local incubators. Most function as incubators without walls. Most of the county offices have started micro loan programs with rules and structures similar to the one described in the Russell neighborhood in Louisville, Kentucky (see chapters 4 and 5). Fifty percent of the initial pool of funds for the programs were contributed by the Hungarian national government and 50 percent by the European Community.

Elmer To'th, chief executive of the local enterprise agency of Heves County, describes his agency. The main office is located in a semimountainous region in the city of Eger, northeast of Budapest. Eger is in a beautiful setting with tourist potential, but with poor highway access for large manufacturing. Because of the high unemployment rate, a large number of people are interested in starting a business. So far the businesses have tended to be very small and low tech. To'th says the majority of small business clients his agency serves are in tourism, local services, agriculture, and production. The agency attempts to emphasize small manufacturing but has few clients in that business. Manufacturing businesses account for about 5 percent of the 2002 clients served in one local office last year (To'th 1995).

Small loans are available for some businesses from the national government, and Heves county has a micro loan program. Generally, finding working capital is difficult. As is true in the United States, most start-up financing comes from the personal resources of the entrepreneurs (Mullin and Armstrong 1983). Heves County's local enterprise assistance agency does not run an incubator building. To'th says, that because of the abundance of municipally owned space, rent is not a critical issue. It is not clear if Heves County understands the benefit of peer support networks that incubators provide.

To'th indicates that a real benefit of the program is that it teaches a large number of local people in this transition environment about business processes. It helps them to comprehend what it means to take risks, respond to markets, and serve customers. Only a small percentage of his 2002 clients will launch successful small businesses with growth potential. Many will start hobby businesses or side jobs. Others may only take a class and never start a business, but all will learn skills valuable for coping in the new environment.

CONCLUSION

The continuous generation and survival of small businesses is important to the success of any community in a free market economy. Small businesses stabilize markets, broaden the local economic base, generate innovation, and create jobs. Because of the special problems associated with the success of small businesses during critical stages of development, intersectoral collaboration to help good businesses through these difficult junctures is justified.

Incubation is a popular process for promoting small business success. It can be used to promote local economic development in general, or to redevelop lagging communities. The incubator building offers advantages to an incubation program in the right situations, but incubation without walls can also be effective. In a formerly Communist country, small business development programs can help people understand how to cope and thrive in a market economy.

Increasingly, partnerships are initiated by the private sector. In addition to this trend, the phrase "private–public partnership" also stresses a point made in the ATI case and alluded to throughout this book: that a goal of the partnership process is to accomplish public policy by perfecting markets, not destroying them. It was mentioned that ATI does not want to use its services to prop up businesses that would fail without its support. ATI even implies that leading a business to ultimate failure does more damage to the economy than if the business had not existed at all. Likewise, a BIDCO or other mixed-sector lender does not want to financially support companies with questionable viability. Capitol BIDCO examines each investment deal at arm's length and applies the principle of "all due diligence" to every financial analysis. The shareholders, be they public, private, or mixed entities, demand this attention to fiduciary responsibility, and Capitol BIDCO will not allow pressure from shareholders to cause it to behave in any other way (Sandstedt 1995). The Hungarian Local Enterprise Assistance Program should keep this point in mind.

In the cases presented in this chapter, public policy is achieved by preparing small businesses to succeed in the marketplace, not by distorting the marketplace.

CHAPTER 7

Intersectoral Collaboration in Ecumenopolis: Crossing Over

Sometimes issues faced by the public are so large that they cannot be resolved through small market adjustments. In some situations, economies of scale are beyond the ability of the marketplace to handle. A good or bad service may be so indivisible that one unit costs millions of dollars, or the positive and negative externalities may be so great that the marketplace breaks down. This is what economists call a "pure public good," one that must be provided by the public sector. Yet, even in these cases, private corporations may participate in ways that facilitate both the free market and future collaboration. Various private activities may spin off. How those private activities are handled can affect the cost and the effectiveness of both public and the private products.

Partly for cultural reasons, and partly because of the size and density of the population, mega development projects are common in East Asia. The preferred approach to urban economic and physical problems and opportunities is to assemble a large parcel of land and develop it intensively. This method is favored because historic subdivision patterns and land costs make parcel assembly difficult. The opportunities for major urban development projects are rare, yet because of population densities, the problems and opportunities that must be addressed by each project are large.

Take, for example, the opportunities created by the inverted-S "ecumenopolis" that is forming in East Asia. Historically, the rim of the Yellow Sea has been a strong cultural and economic region. It became divided several decades ago as some countries pursued socialist directions and some capitalist. Trade, which had grown for two millennia, was greatly reduced.

Despite this division, the cities of the region have continued to grow (Choe 1993). The inverted-S connects the Yellow Sea rim with the Japanese megalopolis. It is the urban corridor running from Beijing to Tokyo via the Yellow Sea coast to Seoul, through Pusan and up the Japanese east coast. While geographically compact, this corridor represents the most developed parts of each of the four countries that it connects, and has a population of over 200 million people, approaching that of the entire United States (Choe 1993).

The existence of the inverted-S has been masked for decades by the political divisions in the area. Yet the collapse of the Soviet Union and the fall of the Berlin Wall have generated the feeling that liberalization of China and North Korea are inevitable. This conclusion has caused people to look at the map of the region with new eyes and imagine new possibilities arising from ancient patterns.

Each country, in its own way, promotes the inverted-S. Japan has extended the Shinkansen bullet train beyond Shimonoseki, which lies across the Korea Strait from Pusan. Korea is planning a similar train from Pusan to Seoul, through the nation's large cities of Taegu and Taejon. Comparable transportation improvements have been discussed for North Korea as a part of any cooperative relationship with South Korea; and "China's Bohai Rim, situated in a most favorable coastal region, facing the Korean Peninsula, and being endowed by rich resources in energy, minerals, and human labor, has witnessed a much higher degree of urbanization than that of the nation as a whole" (Choe 1993, p. 87). The entire region could be covered in two hours by commercial jet and perhaps 10 hours by high speed rail with a tunnel between Pusan, Korea, and Shimonoseki, Japan. With political liberalization, this corridor, with an urban population of over 100 million, could become one of the most powerful economic units in the world (Choe 1993).

This chapter discusses three intersectoral collaborations in two nations on the inverted-S, Korea and Japan. The authors have been following the development of these projects for years, have made site visits, and have participated in conferences focused on analyzing them. All projects are large, physical, urban redevelopment projects in high-density environments with high land costs. Two projects involve reclaiming harbor land and developing an island to avoid high land costs, and all involve several organizations across the public–private spectrum. The first case is at the very heart of the inverted-S, in Inch'on, Korea. Then, two Tokyo region examples examine public entrepreneurship and private statesmanship in the Japanese culture.

KOREA'S PORT, TOURISM, AND INFORMATION TECHNOPOLIS

At the very center of one of the world's most populous and most developed urban corridors is the Seoul metropolitan area with its port city, Inch'on. In the jet age, visitors from the West begin their Korean adventures at Kimp'o Airport. "But in the old days most travelers put in at Inch'on, Seoul's chief seaport" (Lueras and Chung 1989). Until the 1880s, this sleepy fishing village was the only Korean place foreigners were allowed to visit (Lueras and Chung 1989). Westerners were not officially allowed into the "Hermit Kingdom" until 1883. When they did receive royal permission, usually for purposes of trade, Inch'on was the popular port of entry. Today, Inch'on is a busy harbor and Korea's fourth largest city (Lueras and Chung 1989).

For many years after Korea opened the Inch'on gate, this harbor cultivated a lively port-to-port relationship with China, causing a Chinatown to appear along the waterfront (Lueras and Chung 1989). The sea relationship with China may resume in the form of waves of cargo vessels crossing the Yellow Sea, much as they now do between Pusan and Shimonoseki (Hamlin 1994).

The number of ships calling at Inch'on has increased every year. Trans-Yellow Sea trade has increased from 40 TEUs (twenty-foot-equivalent units) in 1990 to 19,195 TEUs in 1994. Cross sea passenger traffic increased from 9,400 to 116,000 in the same period (Chae 1994). But a new airport may mean growing access through the sky. Already, as a consequence of the increased trade, the 38.9 kilometer stretch between Seoul proper and the port of Inch'on has become the most important sea, road, and rail supply route in Korea (Lueras and Chung 1989).

South of Inch'on, along the west coast is ancient Paekche. The Paekche region has a long history of international relations. As early as A.D. 500, Paekche artisans, priests, and architects traveled to central Asia and China, and were greatly influenced by what they learned. Later, in the 500s and 600s, Paekche intelligentsia went to Japan, carrying ideas from the mainland. This infusion of ideas has had a profound influence on Japanese culture to this day (Leuras and Chung 1989).

Development of China

How the west coast of Korea develops depends greatly on what happens politically in China. The future of China is not easy to decipher. Short-term events may be hard to predict, and many setbacks and delays may be part of the process. Yet we can be fairly certain of the long-term direction of China. China will expand economically and increase its contact and trade with the outside world. This growing affluence and external contact will produce further democratization and economic liberalization (Hamlin 1994).

As this happens, Chinese cities will become more powerful locations in the accessibility equation. Korean west coast cities, in turn, will increase their access to economic activity because of their nearness to China. Furthermore, Chinese port cities, such as Tianjin, Lianda, and Dailian, may come to depend on Inch'on for international trade (Hamlin 1994).

New Force for Development in the Region

General Douglas MacArthur's amphibious landing at the turning point of the Korean War hints at the new invasion of trade soon to arrive. MacArthur chose Inch'on as his landing point because the harbor was so shallow and poor for large ships that the enemy would never expect him to land there (Lueras and Chung 1989). Each day as the tide recedes, thousands of acres of mud flats are left visible. Because of the cost and difficulty of assembling land in the metropolitan region, the pressure to reclaim and develop this as developable land has been great. The central location of the port city in the huge urban corridor described above, and the potential created by trade liberalization in the region, induced the national and local governments to act. They decided to mold Inch'on into a leading multimode port city for the next century. This means building perhaps the largest airport in the Northeast Asian quadrasphere, creating the most modern seaport on the Yellow Sea, adding an information teleport to position Inch'on as a center for digital information, promoting conferences and corporate head-quarters—and doing it all on reclaimed mud flats.

Yongjongdo New International Airport in Inch'on is due to be competed in 2005. It is being built on reclaimed land near the island of the same name in Inch'on harbor. Its SST and heavy jet capability, and its central location between China and Japan, will elevate Inch'on as a point of maximum accessibility for a vast international region. The power of this location will grow as China liberalizes its economic policies, and will increase greatly if North Korea does the same (Hamlin 1994).

Furthermore, opening flight paths over Russia draws Inch'on closer to all North American cities and elevates Inch'on's competitiveness vis-à-vis Narita Airport near Tokyo. Continued congestion at Narita contributes to

Yongjongdo's competitive advantage as the hub connecting Asia to North America. This advantage is particularly strong for connecting China to North America (Hamlin 1994).

Inch'on has always been an important freight port, and Yongjongdo New International Airport should be an important air freight facility. The combination of seaport and airport could make Inch'on more than a center of trade with China; it could become a major break-of-bulk point for trade between China and the rest of the world (Hamlin 1994).

The new airport and its economic consequences put enormous developmental pressure on the north side of the city of Inch'on. This facility makes Inch'on a meeting place for goods and ideas. The degree to which Inch'on becomes an important world meeting place depends on the comfort and convenience of the facilities available, and the transportation and communication system connecting the airport to the surrounding region (Hamlin 1994).

One of the first additions to the city to capitalize on the new accessibility will be more meeting and lodging facilities. The market will dictate that these facilities be built, but their quality and location are another matter. They should be close to the airport, with transportation so convenient, simple, and comfortable that a newcomer will easily find and use them. Meeting facilities should be set up to handle small training meetings as well as big conventions (Hamlin and Oranchek 1987). They should be equipped internally with advanced information technology.

The next step in capitalizing on the locational advantage provided by the new airport would be to have electronic communication and information technology infrastructure connecting the airport area to Seoul, Inch'on, and the entire west coast of Korea. It is important to use the airport to jump into the information era. If the airport becomes just a center of air transport without the amenities to make it a world communications center, Korea will lose much of the benefit of this investment. Kenneth Corey states, "Information technologies (IT) should be seriously considered by policy planners in Korea as a direct complement and reinforcement of regional development and local autonomy enhancement" (Corey and Kernan 1993). The power of IT should be harnessed in the service of Korean democratization and localization.

Once the region is established as a meeting place with the latest information technology, it is then positioned to attract corporate branch offices from other parts of the world. Financial services are already well established in Seoul. The combination of corporate branch offices and financial services make it a place where corporate world headquarters could ultimately locate.

Kyongso District of Inch'on City

All of these considerations lead to a discussion of the Kyongso District New Town land reclamation project. This project has the capacity to act as an economic complement to the Yongjongdo New International Airport. It provides space for the facilities previously mentioned, which should naturally partake of the locational advantage of the new airport. The project is being planned on reclaimed land about halfway between the Yongjongdo project and the existing Kimp'o International Airport, which serves Seoul. It is adjacent to the planned transportation corridor connecting Seoul's 11 million people to Yongjongdo. The transportation corridor will have an expressway, rail freight service, and high-speed passenger rail service (Chae 1994).

This public–private partnership venture is a rare opportunity because the transportation links to the airport can be direct and convenient (*Comprehensive Development Plan for the Kyongso District of Inch'on City* 1994). This "new town in town" can become a strong secondary urban center in the Inch'on area. Located on the Kyongso Canal, with a goods distribution center on site, it can also be a critical break-of-bulk point between air, sea, rail, and vehicular transport links (*Comprehensive Development Plan for the Kyongso District of Inch'on City* 1994).

The project is massive, with over 9,202 acres of reclaimed land at the waterfront of Inch'on. It is being developed entirely by a private development company, Dong-Ah Group, one of Korea's largest conglomerates (*chebos*). Dong-Ah is familiar with big projects, having just completed a $3 billion project in Libya. Dong-Ah Construction Industries began reclaiming the tideland in the early 1980s, by constructing a 9,366-meter embankment facing the Yellow Sea (Chae 1994). They carried out the project at their own expense. The government licensed Dong-Ah to reclaim the area in 1980 under a 1979 law. This, in effect, gave Dong-Ah ownership of the mudflats if Dong-Ah reclaimed them. In exchange, the group donated 5,126 acres of the land to the government for public use, and has drawn up the master plan for Kyongso New Town for the other 4,076 acres (Chae 1994). Dong-Ah has the rights to all ownership and profits from the new town after turning infrastructure, parks, and schools over to the local government, approximately 957 acres.

The 1994 master plan, worked out with the affected governments, emphasizes the growth of the target area as a highly advanced technopolis and as a tourist and leisure complex offering a high level of cultural opportunities. The plan sets the following goals:

1. To contribute to the development of the region by building a model international tourist and resort town, thereby improving the quality of life.

2. To promote the potential of Inch'on, which will be connected to the international airport in Yongjongdo, as a gateway to the metropolitan zone.

3. To develop a positive image for Inch'on, thereby making the target area a highlight of the metropolitan zone.

4. To build a distribution center that can serve as a hub of transportation for the eastern region of Northeast Asia and that can augment the existing industrial services of Inch'on, and to provide a residential complex for . . . workers.

5. To create a new vision of city development that takes into consideration private and public goals and interests, and that can serve as a model for future joint development projects between private enterprises and the government (*Comprehensive Development Plan for the Kyongso District of Inch'on City* 1994, p. 6).

The mix of uses planned for the reclamation site offers some internal autonomy and self-sufficiency, yet is tied closely to a world hub of information and transportation. With both high-density and low-density housing near the business complex, the project reduces commutation distances for daily workers. In the Kyongso New Town plan, 31 percent of the land is devoted to a tourist and leisure complex and 8 percent to a distribution center. Residential property occupies 15 percent and business-related property 45 percent. Business property includes a commercial district, a high-tech business complex, a small and medium-sized business R&D complex, an exhibition hall and convention center, a general hospital, a sports facility, a university, schools, parking lots, and parks (*Comprehensive Development Plan for the Kyongso District of Inch'on City* 1994).

The total cost of the development is as follows:

- land assembly   40 million won
- leisure facilities   1.2 trillion won
- other facilities   1.3 trillion won
- contingency   30 billion won

The U.S. dollar is currently worth 777 won. The plan anticipated that land reclamation would be far enough along for construction to begin in 1995 and that the project would be partially completed by 1999, when the leisure facilities opened, and totally completed by 2006.

It should be noted that controversy surrounds the Yongjongdo New International Airport project and, by association, the Kyongso New Town project. Two issues are most salient. The first is the potential for environmental damage caused by such a massive land reclamation project. One can easily imagine the environmental change caused by the filling of 8,000 acres of mudflats. According to some environmental specialists, seashore fields such as those at Yongjongdo serve as buffer zones and filters for ground-water going into the sea. Filling and developing these fields destroys the filter system and works to break down the ocean ecosystem (Young 1993). The second issue is the potential for transportation bottlenecks caused by the location of the airport. Because it uses reclaimed land, the project is located at the extreme northwest corner of the Republic of Korea, just a few miles from the Demilitarized Zone. It is on a man-made island connected by two causeways. People coming from nearly anywhere in the nation by ground transportation must pass through congested parts of Seoul to arrive at this point north of Inch'on. Some estimate that traveling from Yongjongdo to central Seoul could take more than two hours at peak travel times. The plan is for Yongjongdo to be the only international airport serving Seoul, and for Kimp'o to be converted to domestic flights only. Whether this congestion can be avoided depends on the quality of the alternative forms of transportation/communication installed in the area, such as high-speed rail and digital telecommunication (Hwang 1995).

Summary

In the case of the Inch'on West Coast Development Area, the public sector and the private sector foresaw one of history's most powerful economic opportunities at the center of the Northeast Asian ecumenopolis, the 200 million-person, inverted-S urban corridor. In the mid-1980s, both governments and a major development company assumed a large risk by beginning one of the world's largest land reclamation projects in preparation for the development of an international SST jet port and a teleport tech-nopolis new town project that may not be completed until 2005. The national government essentially gave the development company the land for the new town and all potential profits, if the development company would do the work of reclaiming an area twice that size and if it would develop the new town according to a plan worked out with all of the governments involved. The public investment in a large airport, and trans-portation links from the airport to the new town, are strong incentives for the private sector to undertake the project.

This massive, long-term project responds to an enormous opportunity and raises several questions. First, to what extent and how has local government been involved? This project is evolving during a period when

Korea is undertaking a great effort to decentralize power to localities, including the election of local officials. The political environment is changing rapidly. The current, popular mayor of Inch'on is in favor of the project. He had been appointed by the national government, but was recently elected by the people of Inch'on.

Second, to what extent will the project perfect the real estate market in Inch'on city? When a project is carried out by one large developer, what special actions are necessary to integrate the results into the local economy rather than dominate it? Third, to what extent were citizens involved in the project's decisions? Given the scale of the consequences for the nation and the region, what level of local citizen participation is appropriate? Current controversies about the project indicate that at least some groups do not feel "ownership" in the project plan.

These questions will be kept in mind as the project continues to evolve in a fluid governmental and economic environment. The next section examines two projects in Tokyo, the eastern end of the ecumenopolis. Some of the same issues emerge in this nation that carries out large redevelopment projects with large development companies. Yet Japan has a distinct culture and is at a more advanced stage in its economic maturity. Japan's approach to intersector relationships exhibits some unique and interesting variations.

PARTNERSHIPS FOR URBAN REDEVELOPMENT IN JAPAN

Although legally, partnerships do not exist in Japan, a number of highly visible de facto public–private partnerships for urban redevelopment are found throughout the country. Two such mixed endeavors, located in the Tokyo metropolitan area, are described below. They are the Ohkawabata River City 21 project in Tokyo and Omiya Sonic City in suburban Omiya.

In both cases, a public–private partnership was created specifically to carry out a redevelopment project on a given site. Parcel-by-parcel redevelopment is very much the norm in Japanese urban redevelopment efforts. Nevertheless, neither of these endeavors can be described as a simple,short-term organizational partnership between the public sector and the private sector. Both projects have created complex processes involving factors from all parts of the public–private spectrum. In both cases relationships that continue to the present seek to define and pursue the public interest while involving the expertise and motivation of the private investor. Both examples depict how externalities cause market failures that require public intervention.

Ohkawabata River City 21

The purpose of the Ohkawabata River City 21 project, located in Tokyo's Chuo ward, is to help address the worsening central city depopulation problem, caused by high land prices and business expansion. Land prices and rents have been driving out residents, and as the residential population declines, neighborhood amenities and quality of life also decline. At the same time, several islands just offshore from the Chuo ward, where the Sumida River meets Tokyo Bay, are dominated by antiquated industrial uses. Infrastructure there is also aging and not appropriate for residential development. Market stickiness and related externalities are causing land not to be put to its best use or the use desired by public policy. Governmental intervention is called for, but in a way that enhances market mechanisms rather than dominates them.

City officials hope to reestablish residential neighborhoods that are self-contained but well integrated within their central city context. The desire is to return central Tokyo to the level of land use diversity of the Edo period (1603–1867), when people lived close to where they worked and shopped. This goal is enunciated in the Tokyo Metropolitan Long-Range Plan, which seeks to revive *furasato* (our native place). Put more succinctly, the project's goals are threefold: (1) to enhance Chuo ward's central Tokyo location as an amenity; (2) to retain and attract population to the area; and (3) to bring prosperity and activity back to the ward (HUDC 1989).

Chuo ward has a total population of approximately 100,000. Despite a recent steady decline in population, it has several important assets. It is the center of the printing, bookbinding, and food processing industries in Tokyo. It has an extensive waterfront, including frontage along the Sumida River and Tokyo harbor. It possesses a variety of cultural amenities and is located close to the city's commercial hub, Ginza (HUDC 1989).

The River City 21 project site is located at the northern tip of a man-made island near the mouth of the Sumida River on Tokyo's waterfront. It was formerly occupied by a manufacturing plant owned and operated by Ishikawajima-Harima Heavy Industries. The Japanese Housing and Urban Development Corporation (HUDC) and the Mitsui Real Estate Development Company (MREDC) jointly acquired the site in 1979. A large residential development had been proposed for the site in 1972 by the Chuo Ward Redevelopment Council. It was agreed by HUDC and MREDC that such a project was so large, and required enough major public improvements (e.g., roadways, bridges), that it should be treated as a public effort.

That is, it should involve both public and private developers, and should be viewed as having a public purpose (HUDC 1989).

The Tokyo Metropolitan Government's Bureau of Housing and the Tokyo Metropolitan Housing Supply Corporation were invited to join the partnership to lend their expertise in providing housing to a socioeconomically diverse population of anticipated residents. Thus, the partnership came to include private, public, and semipublic participants who worked together to formulate the River City 21 plan. HUDC assumed the lead role in implementation. This semipublic organization both negotiated with the various government agencies involved (Chuo ward, the Tokyo Metropolitan Government, the Ministry of Construction, and others) and coordinated the entire project. MREDC, besides constructing the largest share of the project's housing units, acted as the principal contact with the residents and prospective residents of River City 21 (HUDC 1989).

Project Details

River City 21 includes 2,500 residential units and has a population of approximately 7,500. The housing units are condominiums with a variety of floor plans and range in size from one to four bedrooms. This housing is designed to serve both new residents to the area and former Chuo ward residents who were displaced (HUDC 1989).

The project also includes educational facilities, a variety of retail stores, and cultural facilities. An elementary school, a junior high school, a day-care center, and a community center for children are included. Shopping malls, a seafood restaurant, and Techno Plaza (which includes high-technology business facilities, lodging facilities, and specialty stores) are there as well. Ishikawajima Park, located along the riverfront, is designed to accommodate active and passive recreation, numerous festivals, and other events. Residents can fish, cycle, walk, and jog in the park (HUDC 1989).

Open space and abundant landscaping are an important part of the project's design. Streets are wide, tree-lined, and flanked by terraced embankments. Several pocket parks and play lots are located throughout the development. Open space is provided to create a safety zone to which residents can be evacuated in the event of an emergency (HUDC 1989). This latter feature is common in Japan, where a history of severe earthquakes and resultant fires that have ravaged major cities has prompted officials to take extra precautions. Even the project's flood banks (barriers against tidal waves) are designed to increase open space and enhance water-oriented recreation. Rather than using the traditional steep-walled banks, the partners elected to slope them gently, in order to facilitate access to the river (HUDC 1989).

A new bridge across the Sumida River was built, connecting River City 21 with the mainland. In addition, the Yurakucho Line subway opened its new Tusukishima station to service the area (HUDC 1989).

The total project area is 28.7 hectares (70.88 acres). Of this, 17.2 hectares (42.48 acres) is dedicated to housing and 11.5 hectares (28.40 acres) is occupied by other uses. The floor area ratio for the housing is 4:1. There is parking for 1,600 vehicles, including a robotics facility that takes an automobile on a platform and stores it or recalls it for the owner like a giant jukebox. Landownership of the approximately 42.5-acre housing portion of the project breaks down as follows (HUDC 1989):

Tokyo Metropolitan Government (roads, streams)—14.82 acres

MREDC—11.36 acres

HUDC—6.66 acres

Chuo ward (roads, schools, parks)—5.68 acres

Tokyo Metropolitan Housing Supply Corp.—2.22 acres

Tokyo Metropolitan Government Bureau of Housing—1.72 acres

The housing developers for this project included the four major partners. The number of units developed by each follows (HUDC 1989):

Mitsui Real Estate Development Company—1,170 units (in buildings of fourteen to forty stories)

Housing and Urban Development Corp.—625 units (in buildings of six to thirty-seven stories)

Tokyo Metropolitan Housing Supply Corp.—425 units (in a thirty-seven-story building)

Tokyo Metropolitan Govt. Bureau of Housing—280 units (in buildings of six to twenty stories)

Project History / Schedule

1972—The Chuo Ward Redevelopment Council proposes residential development (in place of existing industrial development) along the banks of the Sumida River under the Ohkawabata Plan.

1979—Ishikawajima-Harima Heavy Industries closes its plant in Chuo Ward, moves to a new location farther from central Tokyo.

—HUDC and MREDC acquire this property jointly; take lead role in implementing the Ohkawabata Plan.

—The Ohkawabata Redevelopment Basic Survey is conducted.

1981—Project's implementation is accelerated as part of the Tokyo Metropolitan Comprehensive Implementation Program (known as the My Town Plan).

1982—The Ministry of Construction approves the Ohkawabata Comprehensive Improvement Promotion Project as a Specific Urban Housing District.

1984—The zoning plan for the Ohkawabata project is formulated, focusing on land use, streets, riverfront development, and building height and bulk.

1985—The environmental impact assessment procedure is initiated.

1986—River City 21 project commences.

1988—Phase I (housing construction) is completed and the units are occupied.

—Techno Plaza construction begins.
—Tsukishima subway station is opened.

1989—Construction along the waterfront is completed.

1992—The new bridge across the Sumida River is completed.

1994—River City 21 project is completed. (HUDC 1989)

Project Financing

The four major partners in the River City 21 project derived their financing from a variety of sources. What follows is a discussion of each of the partner's financial resources (HUDC 1989).

The Tokyo Metropolitan Government Housing Bureau had three sources of financing for this project. Its general source of revenue is the income tax. It also floated a local bond issue to raise funds. In addition, it received grants-in-aid from the Japanese central government.

The Tokyo Metropolitan Housing Supply Corporation is capitalized by the Tokyo Metropolitan Government (the municipal government). It drew on these funds for the project. It also received subsidies from the central government and from the Tokyo Metropolitan Government. The Housing Supply Corporation also used surplus reserve money and borrowed from both public and private sources. Public loans were received from the Tokyo Metropolitan Government and the Housing Loan Corporation, as well as from private financial institutions.

The Housing and Urban Development Corporation is capitalized by investments by the central government and various local governments. It also received a subsidy and grants-in-aid from the central government for the purpose of paying interest on its loans. One loan was received from the Central Government Fund. Others came from private sources, including private financial institutions (Long-Term Credit Bank, life insurance companies, etc.), a housing and urban development bond, and a special housing bond.

The fourth partner, Mitsui Real Estate Development Company, is investor-owned. It used three different types of bonds: a corporate bond, a convertible bond, and a bond with a preemptive right. In addition, MREDC received a loan from the public entity known as the Housing Loan Bank, and private loans from banks and life insurance companies.

Tax breaks also played an important role in encouraging the River City 21 redevelopment project. While no special tax package was assembled for this project, several general tax subsidies offered by the Japanese government to promote such activities were available. One such tax provision permits the accelerated depreciation of new assets acquired upon the transfer of original assets to HUDC for one of its housing construction projects. In this case, Ishikawajima-Harima Heavy Industries transferred its assets at the River City 21 site to HUDC and acquired a new plant elsewhere, taking advantage of this tax break. Ishikawajima-Harima Heavy Industries received a similar tax break when it sold a portion of its assets to MREDC, under a law that encourages the deconcentration of industry in central Tokyo.

Redevelopment projects in densely developed areas receive preferential treatment relative to several national and local taxes under the Urban Redevelopment Law. Because River City 21 is a redevelopment project, its developers enjoyed relief of various types from national personal income, registration and license, stamp, and corporation taxes. Relief was also granted from local real estate acquisition, business income, property, business office, and special landholding taxes.

Implications for Public–Private Partnership for Urban Redevelopment

While "partnership," per se, has no legal definition in Japan, the River City 21 case affords an example of a de facto partnership among public, quasipublic, and private entities that carries forward a clear public purpose and at the same time yields benefits to all participants. River City 21 fulfills, in part, the objective of both Chuo ward and the Tokyo Metropolitan Government to bring residential development back to the central city. It has carried out this purpose by overcoming some of the market impediments often associated with inner city environments. The process freed up potentially valuable land by inducing a major industrial user to move out of the congested core. It assembled and readjusted land to make it more usable; it provided important infrastructure, including bridges, parks, and a subway line, in addition to upgrading all of the necessary urban systems; and it induced private development through financial incentives and tax breaks. In short, the project promoted the public interest in a way that was sensitive to public health, safety, and quality of life, and it did so while enhancing the function of urban real estate markets and the systems for future collaboration.

A major private housing developer and the most relevant public and semipublic organizations contributed resources and worked together to acquire land; develop a plan; coordinate the provision of major physical infrastructure facilities; construct housing; and provide educational, cultural, recreational, and commercial amenities. Each entity had its own role to play and contribution to make to the whole project, and it was all coordinated in an effective and synergistic manner.

The public benefit in this case is derived from the development of a well-planned urban community that encourages the return to the central city of people from a range of socioeconomic levels. This warrants the participation of the three public and quasipublic members of the partnership. The private-sector partner benefits, as well, from the collection of tax subsidies that it receives, the public facilities that enhance the value of its investment, and the profit from selling its share of the housing units.

In many respects this is a very "clean" form of partnership, in that the financial arrangements are not particularly complex; the roles and responsibilities of the participants are well defined; and there is effective leadership by HUDC. This latter element is of particular importance. Capable leadership has been widely cited as a key ingredient to successful public–private partnership (Bertsch 1984; Porter and Sweet 1984; Levitt 1987). HUDC, itself a quasipublic entity or public–private partnership, is especially well suited to play the leadership role in this case. It enjoys an image of neutrality and can use this effectively in conducting negotiations among partners and coordinating project operations. HUDC also possesses an all-important understanding of the internal workings of both the public and private sectors. This is invaluable to keeping the partnership balanced (Landis 1990).

Omiya Sonic City

Omiya Sonic City is a combined business and cultural urban redevelopment project located in the city of Omiya, Saitama prefecture, in metropolitan Tokyo. In addition to its English connotation, the word "sonic" is employed because the letters that constitute it represent the key partners and the principal functions of the project: S=Saitama; O=Omiya; N=Nihon Seimei (Nippon Life Insurance Company); I=industry, international; C=culture, convention.

Project Details

The building is the first super skyscraper to be built in the prefecture and in the northern suburbs of Tokyo. It includes a 209-room hotel; office space; retail shops; meeting rooms; banquet facilities; athletic clubs; restaurants; a 2,505-seat convocation hall; a 496-seat convocation hall; an international conference room; and parking for 2,750 vehicles.

The site has a total of 2.23 hectares (5.5 acres). The building covers 1.36 hectares (3.35 acres), and the remainder is divided as follows: open space, 0.39 hectare (0.96 acre); a park, 0.28 hectare (0.70 acre); and a bus terminal, 0.2 hectare (0.49 acre). The site is adjacent to Omiya Station, which boasts 9 railway lines and 500,000 passengers per day, thus giving users of Sonic City ready access to mass transit. A drawing of the site and the building complex is shown in Figure 3.

Project Purposes/Partnership Arrangement

The purposes of the Omiya Sonic City project are fourfold. First, it was designed to establish a "growth pole" in suburban Omiya, in an effort to enhance economic development in the prefecture. Second, it was intended to create a cultural center for Saitama prefecture, which is expected to attain a maximum population of over 7 million. Third, Sonic City was created to promote interregional and international exchanges of all kinds. Finally, it was intended that the project become a symbol of the prefecture and its urban core.

These were the objectives of the public–private partnership that was formed to develop Sonic City. The principal partners were Saitama prefecture, Nihon Seimei, and Fujita Corporation. These entities adopted a partnership structure that the Japanese call a "private-sector-utilization scheme." Essentially, the roles of the partners were very clear and distinct. The prefecture was responsible for planning and design, and the private partners were responsible for implementation (i.e., construction and management). Thus, the public sector was utilizing the private sector to put its plans into action. This makes for a very straightforward approach to public–private partnership, one in which both duties and benefits are very apparent. In this case, the prefecture achieved the public objectives delineated above, and Nihon Seimei and Fujita reaped the economic benefits from a massive commercial development.

The details of this project and the partnership arrangement are worthy of note. The effort began with the establishment of the objectives of the project by the prefecture, with input from the public. Thus, public expectations for

Figure 3
Omiya Sonic City, Saitama Prefecture, Japan

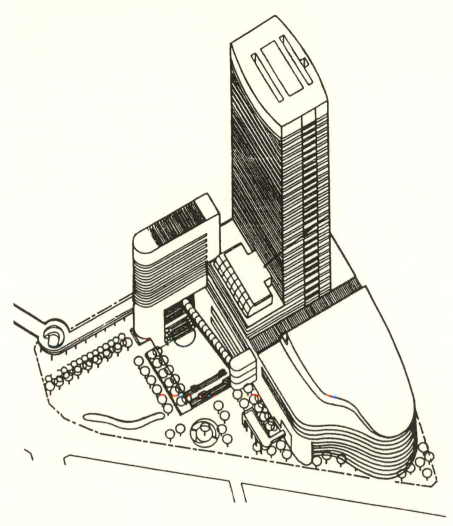

the effort were established up front via a democratic process. These public objectives for Sonic City were then formalized in a request for proposals that was disseminated to interested private-sector developers. Private proposals were submitted and reviewed, with selection of the winning proposal based solely on the proposer's ability to achieve the stated public objectives in the most desirable fashion. This is quite different from the standard approach in the United States, which focuses on price competition. Price is irrelevant here, because the successful proposer will build the project with its own funds.

In the case of Sonic City, Nihon Seimei and Fujita Corporation won the competition and constructed the building with their own money, at a cost of 36.26 billion yen. Saitama prefecture owns the land and leases it to Nihon Seimei. Nihon Seimei owns the private portion of the building (hotel, retail shops, etc.), while the prefecture owns the public portion of the building (convention halls, international conference room, etc.), which it acquired from the Fujita Corporation (the construction company). In this way, the prefecture and Nihon Seimei share the building in a partitioned joint ownership. Fujita recouped its costs through the sale of public areas to the prefecture. Omiya Sonic City opened its doors in April 1988.

Implications for Public–Private Partnership for Urban Redevelopment

Unlike River City 21, which established a quasipublic entity as its leader, this project was clearly led by the public sector, in the form of Saitama prefecture. While the prefecture does not enjoy the perception of neutrality that the Housing and Urban Development Corporation of Japan does, the way in which the Sonic City partnership arrangement was structured makes this less important. In effect, the prefecture established the vision for the project and then solicited a suitable private partner that could help make it happen. In this way, a combination of public vision and private money and know-how yielded a successful project.

The process employed in the Sonic City case worked to ensure that public purpose/public benefit was the focus of the project. The private partners benefited as well; however, there was never a possibility that the objectives of the prefecture and its residents would be lost in the scramble for profitability. Two features of the process were particularly important to achieving an equitable partnership: (1) active participation by local residents in the visioning process and (2) the use of proposal solicitation to determine the private partners. Public participation helped to ensure that the government was not entering into a partnership that it need not have entered (Gunyou 1990), and that those who would be most affected by the final project had a say in planning it. The proposal solicitation process served as a vehicle for communicating the public vision for the project, thus making the terms of the partnership very clear; identifying only those potential private partners who were willing and able to carry that vision to implementation; and generally affording the partners an opportunity to assess one another before entering into an agreement.

One other interesting aspect of the Omiya Sonic City partnership is the joint public–private ownership of the building. This arrangement not only serves to put the appropriate entity in control of various physical, social, and economic functions of the facility, but it also tends to perpetuate the partnership beyond the financing and construction phases. This aspect is ripe with potential in several ways. First, it permits private and public activities within the building to enhance one another, thereby improving the probability of success for both over what it might be if they stood alone. Second, it literally and figuratively invests both partners in the continued success of the project. Third, it could be argued that this arrangement affords greater flexibility to the project, making it more resilient to changing conditions over time. Finally, if the partnership continues to be amicable, it could lay the groundwork for other joint ventures between the parties as they learn to respect each other's strengths and perspectives.

Lessons for Successful Partnerships from Ecumenopolis

Attempting to transfer socioeconomic technologies from one country to another is always tricky. This is particularly true of such technologies used in countries like Korea and Japan, which are homes to ancient cultures and homogeneous populations. East Asian society is oriented to group undertakings and general cooperation. Thus, collaboration seems to come more naturally than it does in the United States.

Japanese culture carries collaboration a step farther. Partnership in Japan does not need to be legalized; it merely exists as an unconstrained aspect of human relationships. Furthermore, the public sector in Japan enjoys greater respect than does its counterpart in the United States, which is widely regarded as being inferior to the private sector. The impact of the latter circumstance on successful public–private partnership should not be taken lightly. Effective intersectoral collaboration requires mutual trust and respect among the partners.

Intersectoral collaboration in Japan has its own constraints. In some unusual ways, the division between the public sector and the private sector continues to be more distinct than in Korea or other countries. For example, construction labor unions tend to be divided between those that work on public projects and those that work on private projects. Each jealously guards its own turf, making the combining of public and private property more difficult. Even the construction of private buildings in the air rights of public expressways is rare in Japan as a result of this issue. The use of eminent domain to accumulate land and update property lines is difficult because of the strong desire to keep family-owned property in the family. And official communication must take place between individuals of equal rank, making the decision process long and bureaucratic.

As a result of these difficulties, urban redevelopment tends to be a very slow process, carried out one project at a time. Within these projects, what looks like a simple financial partnership between a public or quasipublic entity and a private corporation is really a long, careful negotiation process that attempts to balance a multitude of public and private interests. Not the least important of the partners is the *dai-yon* (fourth) sector (Hagiwara 1991), the citizens and landowners in the project area, who are afforded significant power in the negotiation process because of the reluctance to use condemnation or otherwise force businesses or residents from their locations. Partnership in Japan is a process of consensus building.

Despite the differences among the three projects in the two countries discussed in this chapter, there are lessons that have universal relevance. Some of them are described below.

1. Partnership arrangements should be clear. Each party should carry out the roles to which it is best suited. Roles should be made explicit from the beginning.

2. One of the partners must assume an unambiguous leadership role. Partnership maintenance requires clear direction, negotiation, consensus building, diplomatic management of operations, and unswerving attention to the mutual benefit of the partners. Strong, balanced leadership can provide these. Partners that are neither public nor private (i.e., quasipublic, nonprofit) can be especially attractive for the leadership role due to their perceived neutrality. However, as demonstrated in the Omiya Sonic City case, distinctly public or private partners can lead effectively, given an appropriate partnership process and structure and a clear statement of the public interest.

3. The residents of the community to be redeveloped should be involved in the process of articulating the public purpose of the partnership. This lends additional credence to the public side of the mutual benefit equation that is so crucial to equitable public–private partnerships. The public purpose is less likely to be lost or ignored in the partnership-building and project implementation phases of the process.

4. Joint ownership of the final product of the partnership carries some distinct advantages. This is discussed in the Sonic City case. Joint ownership in both a legal and an emotional sense is required.

NOTE

Information on Omiya Sonic City was derived from various materials provided by officials of Saitama prefecture as well as a site visit by both authors.

CHAPTER *8*

Implications for the Development Professions: Long-Range Planning for Rapid Change

The trends in the relationship between the public sector and the private sector described in this book lead to several conclusions about the theory, research, and practice of local development planning. The trends say something about the organization of the development profession, professional ethics, future career paths for students, and future research agendas for academicians. The implications are increasingly worldwide in scope (Hamlin and Lyons 1993). This chapter discusses the possible effects of an economy without walls on planning and development theory, including consequences for professional ethics.

COMPREHENSIVE PLANNING

Students of urban planning philosophy have always valued comprehensiveness and interdisciplinary unity. An understanding of the synergy of urban forces and the need for synthesizing skills have been hallmarks of the urban planning profession worldwide. One important trend concerning unity in urban planning is the increasing collaboration between the public sector and the private sector for mutual benefit. In the past, the unity of town planning has referred to the interplay of professionals such as planners, civil engineers, surveyors, and designers in the creation of public policy for cities. Now that economic systems are increasingly mixed, the expertise and biases of the business professional must be factored into the interdisciplinary equation. In addition, a new, distinct profession, management of third-sector organizations, has emerged (Hamlin and Lyons 1993).

Long-Range Planning

The planning profession has always placed great value on having a long-range perspective. Once constructed, the built environment tends to last in excess of thirty years, sometimes hundreds of years. Decisions made today shape the human environment for a long time, it is argued, and city plans should look at least thirty years into the future. In a dynamic world driven by changing markets and technology, thirty years seems like a long time. Planners are often frustrated in their attempts to induce people to think about the future and then to follow long-range plans once they are established. Many have thrown up their hands and said that planning must take place incrementally, one project at a time.

On the one hand, the trend toward mixed economies makes predicting long-term futures increasingly difficult. Local markets change rapidly in response to market conditions around the globe. Traditional planners find it increasingly frustrating to see world economic trends far beyond their control render long-range land use plans irrelevant. If formulated too rigidly, community plans based on interactions with private firms, as described in the previous chapters, might have even less relevant longevity (Hamlin and Lyons 1993).

On the other hand, a greater understanding of the power of the market-place points out the importance of defining broad guidelines for the future. Long-range planning becomes more important, not less, in a rapidly changing environment. Market forces can overrun long-range plans whether or not a community engages in public–private partnerships. In fact, one advantage of working in concert with private entities is that it helps a community keep its finger on the pulse of world market trends (Hamlin and Lyons 1993).

So what is the solution? Public–private partnerships should not shorten the time frame for future planning. These trends should change the nature of long-range plans. Plans must be flexible enough to respond to market changes. They need to concentrate less on describing the details of desired static futures. They need to focus more on laying ground rules within which market forces can operate. If one delineates broad parameters, market forces fill in the details of the long-range plans over time, while simultaneously promoting the public interest (Hamlin and Lyons 1993).

This approach demands a mind-set different from traditional planning. It requires a greater level of comfort in dealing with uncertainty. Dealing with uncertainty does not mean throwing up one's hands and riding the roller coaster. It means continuously calculating and recalculating probabilities and responding to risks. The appropriate mentality may be closer to that of a stock market investor than of an architect. Though the stock market moves quickly, investors with a long-range plan succeed (Hamlin and Lyons 1993).

Citizen Participation

If the focus of planning is to nudge the private sector in the right direction, rather than to implement static, detailed futures, then citizens can exert three types of input into the future direction of their community. One type of influence is participation in the electoral process, including voting, participating in election campaigns and communicating with elected officials. A second type is through participation in citizen boards and commissions, community and neighborhood groups, third-sector entities, and volunteer organizations. The third type is as a consumer in the marketplace, casting dollar votes (Hamlin and Lyons 1993).

In the 1960s, when the planning profession first wrestled with political relevance, it intertwined the first and second types of citizen action discussed above. Now planners must also integrate the third, the dollar vote, into their thinking. An economist uses the concept of the dollar vote to describe how consumer demand affects outcomes in society. The idea is that some activities, projects and services must be allowed to sink or swim, based on the level of consumer demand.

While these forms of citizen involvement may still not be adequate, the variety offers an array of messages to the public sector. The electoral process communicates to the public sector the nature of the leadership the community wants, in terms of personality, beliefs, and competency. Citizen participation on lay boards and commissions should delineate and prioritize broad goals for the community as well as feelings about whether the community is moving toward those goals. As a part of this process, it should differentiate between futures that are desirable and those that are critical or imperative (Hamlin and Lyons 1993).

The detailed evolution of the community is not something that planners can dictate. The community evolves from the interplay of market forces, as citizens cast dollar votes every day. Government intervenes in the market to move the private sector's behavior toward desired future community goals. These nudges often take the form of public–private partnerships. Critical or imperative outcomes, defined through citizen input and the policy-making process, may require government to mandate or outlaw some private behavior (Hamlin and Lyons 1993).

STRATEGIC PLANNING

As discussed in Sorkin et al. (1986), strategic planning is not always labeled "strategic," and is not easy to define. It distinguishes itself from other kinds of planning by a specific methodology, and the following key characteristics:

- It is a focused process that concentrates on selected issues.
- It explicitly considers resource availability.
- It assesses strengths and weaknesses.
- It considers major events and changes occurring outside the organization or jurisdiction.
- It is action oriented, with a strong emphasis on practical results.

According to this definition, strategic planning is distinct from the long-range planning described in the first section in that it focuses on specific issues. Yet strategic planning must start with a set of long-range goals and guidelines. It can be viewed as a midrange approach to translating those goals into actions. Even broad policy goals must be periodically reassessed in a rapidly changing, market-oriented system. Extensive citizen involvement in the goal assessment process is a key component of community strategic planning. Identifying actions that push the private sector toward the accomplishment of public goals should also involve citizens.

PLANNING AND POLITICS

The trend toward public–private partnerships has significant implications for representative democracy and for the relationship of planning to politics. Many of these implications are valid whether referring to advanced democracies, developing countries, or nations recently under Communist rule. The viability of an electoral democratic system depends on the ability of voters to receive and assimilate information relevant for judging the performance of their elected officials. Even in very open political systems, citizens do not have time to understand all the issues facing their community. They naturally focus on a few (Hamlin and Lyons 1993).

Incumbent political leaders interested in reelection must maintain a positive public image by controlling the public's salient issue agenda. One strategy for influencing the public agenda is to focus attention on a few visible, successful projects or programs for which the incumbent can take responsibility. They should be activities that voters easily understand and relate to, and with which the politico's name is clearly linked. Typically successful short term "brick and mortar" projects serve best.

Politicians naturally want to control such projects or programs and to keep relationships simple, in order to ensure and claim credit for success. Carrying out public policy indirectly by building partnerships with private organizations and/or intervening in markets diminishes both control and identification. It may increase political risks while reducing the ability to take credit for success. Some political leaders therefore resist this trend toward mixed implementation strategies (Hamlin and Lyons 1993).

On the other hand public–private projects may reduce the pressure on the public budget. With the adoption of Proposition 13 in California in 1979, a state-level tax revolt began to spread across the country and has since spread to the national level. This has had a dramatic effect on the ability of governments to raise revenues. In many places throughout the United States, taxes can be increased only by public referendum. Several states have substantially reduced property taxes and restricted the uses to which the revenues they generate may be put. Other sources have also been severely restricted. At the same time, the public's demand for government services continues unabated.

In the midst of this crisis, governments have been casting about for alternative means of financing the services and physical infrastructure they are still expected to provide. Two mechanisms, in particular, have emerged as popular options: privatization and user charges and fees. Privatization is what many people think of when the term "public–private partnership" is used. Yet privatization in its purest form is not about partnerships at all. It denotes either a strictly contractual relationship between the sectors or the complete abdication of a public responsibility to the private sector. It lacks the mutual benefit aspect of intersectoral collaborations. This may help to explain, in part, why privatization does not always stand up well to evaluations of its equity. Privatization is certainly no panacea, for there are certain activities that remain best carried out by the public sector.

User fees have become increasingly important as an alternative source of public revenue (Zorn 1991). Their popularity stems, in part, from their ability to satisfy the benefit principle of equity (i.e., that those who receive the benefit of a public service should pay for it) (Rafuse 1991). They have also been championed as an alternative to privatization because they permit the charging of public prices, as opposed to private, which is more appropriate for services with characteristics of public goods (Zorn 1991).

Public–private partnerships also can be utilized as vehicles for providing public services and infrastructure in times of fiscal constraint. The public infrastructure and government-provided services that we have come to depend upon represent mutual benefit for both sectors. Yet, the scenario described above has placed the public sector in a classic "Catch 22." If the private sector needs and wants these services, then it must accept its share of the responsibility for providing them. Because universal privatization cannot yield the most efficient or effective answer to the problem, a collaborative capitalism becomes all the more attractive as an alternative. If public–private partnerships take place on a level playing field, the public sector can continue either to set the agenda or to monitor it for conformance to the public interest.

An interesting emerging political reality of American society enters the picture as well. Increasing diversity, and the widely differing perspectives and interests it brings, along with a broadly perceived failure by government to solve pressing societal problems, has brought about a mistrust of the public sector and its ability to define a "public interest" and effectively represent it. Davidoff (1965) has suggested that there are actually many "public interests." thus, the government may merely be representing one of these, as is suggested by the political economy literature on city "growth machines" (Logan and Molotch 1987) and by regime theory.

Whether or not one embraces these theories, the fact is that today the government is often just one of the parties to negotiations regarding urban redevelopment issues (Fulton 1989). A variety of public, private, and third-sector interest groups are typically involved. This suggests that public–private partnerships are being formed out of necessity as the formerly clear-cut boundaries between the sectors continue to blur. It also suggests that the only way to provide needed public physical infrastructure and services effectively and equitably may be via intersectoral arrangements.

PROFESSIONAL AND BUSINESS ETHICS

Planning and development that utilize complex relationships between government and companies challenge the moral and ethical fiber of both the legal and the cultural system. As government uses its advantages to promote corporate profits, and hires businesses to perform government functions, the potential for conflict of interest increases. Greater trust and new forms of oversight need to be developed (Hamlin and Lyons 1993).

For years, Americans have been used to thinking in terms of an adversarial relationship between business and government. The concept of "privatism," a term first coined by Sam Bass Warner, Jr., holds that the private sector should be the engine that drives the American economy, and that government should intervene only as a referee to settle private disputes (Barnekov et al. 1989). This largely nineteenth-century paradigm is still strongly ingrained in the American psyche. It has been modified somewhat by thinking and events of the twentieth century, not the least of which are Keynesian economics and Roosevelt's New Deal programs, which served to expand government's role to that of "protector of the public interest" and the myriad functions that title implies. In recent years, this latter paradigm has come under renewed attack.

Regardless of which ideology holds primacy, however, the underlying theme of private-sector actors as participants and public-sector entities as watchdogs persists. Many would argue that this juxtaposition of sectors has served us quite well over time. Yet the rise of intersectoral collaboration has challenged this paradigm, causing the "Chicken Littles" of society to proclaim that the sky is indeed falling: that, depending upon their chosen ideology, either "the fox has been left to guard the henhouse" or "big government is once again interfering where it doesn't belong."

These attitudes assume that the sectors are incapable of working together without abusing one another, which will be a self-fulfilling prophecy as long as they view themselves, and are viewed by society, as adversaries. Adversarial relationships connote hostility, one-upmanship, and other negative qualities that preclude true partnership. The question arises as to whether this kind of interaction between the major sectors is crucial to an independent, ethical, equitable, and profitable society.

Were we to adopt a new paradigm in which private-sector actors viewed themselves not merely as captains of the economy whose mission it is to generate as much profit as the law will allow, but also as statesmen who are genuinely concerned with the well-being of society, and public-sector actors perceived themselves not only as defenders of the public interest, but also as entrepreneurs interested in advancing societal well-being to new heights, the issues raised above would all but become moot. There would be ample common ground upon which to build a consensus for adopting a code of ethics that both recognizes the new realities and preserves time-honored values. That common ground would be mutual benefit embedded in a concern for society as a whole. Given the rapid and dramatic movement toward intersectoral partnership described in this book, this new paradigm becomes less of a utopian vision and more of a practical necessity.

John Forester (Krumholz and Forester 1990, p. 253) has argued that ethics in planning should "refer to a capacity to argue about what to do, to a capacity to think about, evaluate, and judge alternative courses of action." This capacity presupposes dialogue, a dialogue that seldom exists in public and private interactions. The only way to achieve such dialogue lies in the recognition by the sectors of their mutual interests. This can then serve as the foundation for dialogue, negotiation, and ultimately, consensus. Interaction of this nature can help to ensure that conflicts of interest are eliminated.

Past experimentation with mixed systems illustrates that while ethical problems do arise, the challenge strengthens professional and business ethics. These programs open each sector to the scrutiny of the other and induce the actors, and the public at large, to think about related ethical issues.

EQUITY

Anytime a public–private partnership is established, there should be concern that it is equal and that the benefits derived are widely and fairly distributed. Too often the public sector operates at a disadvantage in these arrangements. This is the case, in part, because government typically is poorly schooled in the ways of business and, therefore, is at the mercy of its private partner(s) in negotiating the terms of the relationship (Landis 1990). This suggests another contributing factor: the private sector partner(s) is(are) characteristically not conditioned to think communally. Under such circumstances, it is little wonder that certain private parties tend to fare better than the public as a whole. This problem can be partially mitigated by educating government as to how business works and how businesspeople think (Landis 1990; Lyons and Hamlin 1991). In this way, government can operate as a full and equal partner, able to negotiate for the public benefit in an effective manner. This also implies that government will behave as a private partner would by thoroughly analyzing the fiscal and economic ramifications of any proposed partnership (Gunyou 1990). An effort must also be made to educate business as to its civic duty, and the fact that it is possible to do both "good" and "well."

Another way to facilitate greater equity in public–private partnerships is to involve the community's residents in the process of assessing the public benefit to be derived and developing the public vision. This approach has two distinct advantages: (1) it helps to clarify and reinforce the public sector's position in negotiations, and (2) it gives those who will be most affected by the results of the partnership an opportunity to veto the deal if it is a bad one. As John Gunyou (1990, p. 11) has stated it, "The golden rule of public/private partnerships is: It is not necessary that the city be involved in all development projects."

HISTORY AND THE FUTURE

These trends in planning theory are not totally new. In the United States, where public planning has remained weak, planners have always been held inferior to the forces of the market. They have had to learn to use market forces to implement plans. The urban renewal programs of the early 1960s represented a significant trial of this approach, and urban renewal authorities were important third-sector organizations (Hamlin and Lyons 1993).

In the face of this formal weakness, some planners have clung to their static long-range master plans, claiming that the plans need only periodic review. Others have abandoned comprehensive long-range planning in favor of an incremental project orientation. In Japan, for example, planning seems always to have been more project oriented than in the United States. The tendency toward project-oriented public–private partnerships intensified in the United States during the economic downturn of the 1970s. The Urban Development Action Grant program was probably typical of the approach of that period. The trend accelerated in the United States shortly after 1983. The recession of that year, the worst since the Great Depression, became the mother of invention for new styles of plan implementation in the United States (Hamlin and Lyons 1993).

Years of experience indicate that at the project level, innovative liaisons between public goals and private goals can be established, such that neither side abuses the relationship. The economy without walls will challenge our system of ethics and political oversight. Yet the result may be to strengthen rather than weaken them. The real challenge is to move beyond the project level and to formulate a theory of long-range interdisciplinary planning and development that responds to this increasingly mixed environment. This will take more time.

CHAPTER 9

Implications for Urban and Regional Analysis: Data Without Walls

These new economic realities, and resultant trends in planning and development theory and practice, allude to the need for a new kind of information and analysis system for planning and municipal management. Information is power. To ensure the success of the new order of relationships between the public sector and the private sector, municipal officials need a new kind of knowledge to translate public goals into feasible and implementable solutions. Local public officials need information to determine appropriate inducements to private initiative and investment, and to successfully forecast the impact of those inducements, so as to develop strategies for implementing public–private partnerships. Private investors also desire better information about the community; and citizens must be better informed for democracy to function in this more complex environment.

This new information and analysis system should include (1) the collection of new kinds of data, (2) different methods for organizing data elements, (3) faster and easier access to information with built-in analytical tools, (4) new projection and prediction techniques, and (5) models with "what if" scenarios based on predictive theories. To build this new information and analysis system, we need empirical research to test theory, and fresh conceptual insights to build new theory. How the economy without walls between the public and the private sectors affects each of these will be discussed in this chapter.

DATA

In the past, local data collection by planners and other municipal officials has focused on providing the best possible statistical snapshot of a community's existing situation. Information has taken the form of a set of categorized, discrete elements organized in hierarchical fashion. Key information has included population, economic, and social data, and information about physical facilities.

Computer technology has increased local capacity to build enormous databases, thus greatly sharpening the level of detail of that snapshot. Graphic pictures and videos can now be embedded in the database. Municipal tax rolls now include visuals of the property along with basic data. This burgeoning capacity has been beneficial to local planning and development. Yet, notwithstanding new bells and whistles, most large databases remain electronic filing cabinets. They maintain the hierarchical structure of their manual predecessors. They contain more detailed versions of the same information, updated at approximately the same frequency (Hamlin and Lyons 1993).

Public officials like to operate in a closed analysis system that excludes the private sector or assumes that private entities will simply follow public plans when the proper regulation is applied. A more iterative relationship between the public and the private sectors expands the need for data for at least four reasons. First, public policy implementers need more information about private firms, in general, and about firms with which they are dealing, in particular. Examples are information about business finance, market trends and market share, prices, and cost structures. Second, private firms, in their role as socially responsible citizens, interacting as partners with the public sector, need better information about their community (Hamlin et al. 1990).

Third, the fast pace of complex, dynamic, market-oriented systems means information must be updated more frequently than in the past. The decennial census is useful for traditional population projections. It is less useful when a community's future is affected by a major public–private partnership project. Daily changes in interest rates may alter the feasibility of that project, making the community's future direction uncertain (Hamlin and Lyons 1993). Fourth, effective political oversight in this mixed environment is more difficult. To ensure responsiveness in a democratic society, better data must be available to both bureaucrats and citizens. This requires special information to monitor projects and programs, greater accuracy of that information, and openness in its dissemination (Hamlin and Lyons 1993).

UTILIZATION OF DATA

Use of information lags our capacity to store it. Most big databases are underutilized because of real or perceived difficulty in information retrieval. While the "Worldwide Web" greatly increases our capacity to plug into more databases, the use of that information by the public is not improved. The ever-increasing size of databases, the need for both public and private access, and growing use of data by noncomputer professionals means better access systems are essential to make the information available and meaningful to a broad range of people. Several considerations related to usefulness are (1) ease of use; (2) relational vs. hierarchical access, (3) the user's ability to ask the right questions and, therefore, seek the right information, (4) the user's aptitude for choosing and carrying out the right analysis with the raw data, (5) the capacity to display the results in a useful way, and (6) protection of proprietary information (Hamlin and Lyons 1993). These issues are discussed below.

Ease of Use

The first issue is ease of access. At this stage in history, no reason remains for database access to be the exclusive realm of computer professionals. Information should be at the fingertips of all those authorized to use it. The data should be available to both public and private users. Information should be on-line to any microcomputer with a modem or other workstation connection. Furthermore, the mainframe server should link to standard networks so as to avoid long-distance calls. Users should be able to call a local telephone number that acts as a "gate" to the network that connects to one or more mainframes. Many communities still do not have this capacity.

The set of commands required to tie into the server, access the database, download data, and manipulate and display information should be small and self-explanatory. Software that allows these tasks is called the front-end system. The front-end system should be as user-friendly as possible. Front-end systems for the Internet, such as Mosaic and Netscape, are improving rapidly to allow individuals to connect to large public databases. Unfortunately, few large databases have easy front-end systems once they are connected. Instructions are often obtuse. Mainframe databases are sometimes slow to respond to requests for information because of the large amount that must be searched. Mainframe front-end systems seldom offer more than the ability to call up and download information, even for the experienced user.

Fortunately, microcomputer storage capacity is expanding rapidly. Installing large databases on hard disk, CD ROM, and other local mass storage devices is now possible, and reduces the need to communicate with a mainframe computer. Still, a front-end system, adequately easy for the novice computer user, is necessary but difficult to find.

Relational Access

One can enter and move through a database in a variety of ways. A hierarchical system operates like a tree or river system. One chooses branches or subcategories at each decision node, seeking smaller and smaller categories until a particular quantitative value or piece of information is encountered. This approach is the easiest to understand for most people (Hamlin and Lyons 1993).

A relational database establishes a "record" at the end of each branch of the hierarchy, with each record containing more than one parcel of information. If similar information is arranged in an identical format across records, a "field" is created. An example is a database with information about each housing unit in a community. Assume the database has a record for each housing unit with two fields, one listing the number of square feet and the other, the number of persons living there. When constructed in this way, information that cuts across the hierarchy can be extracted by accessing the values in a selected field for some set of records. (For instance, to determine the total square feet for all housing units in a community, sum the values in the "square feet" field for each record. Or, to list all housing units with more than four residents, search all records for values higher than four in the "persons" field, and sort the records.) Fields that can be manipulated in this way are active or "hot" fields (Hamlin and Lyons 1993).

This is a better system for quick retrieval of information and for enabling analysis across an entire community. However, this kind of database is more complex than the simple tree format. It requires a front-end system that demands greater expertise on the part of the user, or greater help embedded in the system. It mandates more computer storage, central processing unit time, and on-line time. Both the advantages and disadvantages of a relational database increase as the number of hot, or active, fields in each record is increased (Hamlin and Lyons 1993).

Geographic Information

Geographic information systems (GIS) add "location" as another element in the data structure. In essence, a GIS is a relational database where each record is associated with a coordinate or set of coordinates on a geographic map. This adds tremendously to the computer's processing and storage requirements. Creating a local GIS requires several steps. The first is establishing the geographic "elements" or set of coordinates. The second is formulating the relational database. The third step is linking the geographic elements to the records in the database (Huxhold 1991).

This only brings us back to the level of creating a snapshot of the community, albeit a snapshot with great detail, displayed in a visual mode. Few planning offices get much beyond this stage, although the real value of the GIS system is not employed until the next step, when the database is used for analysis. This will be discussed in the next section. A simple analysis illustration is provided using the example of the previous section. When the set of housing units with greater than four residents is determined, and their geographic element is referenced, maps can be generated that indicate the pattern of their location.

GISs are increasingly powerful but not yet user-friendly. Operating most systems requires significant training and experience. Equipment is expensive. Since hardware and software are quickly outmoded, the annualized cost of an urban system is often prohibitive.

Basic Analysis and Graphics Capability

Having retrieved appropriate data, an effective front-end system should be able to carry out basic analysis without transferring the data to other analysis programs. Examples of this simple analysis are (1) restating all financial data in current dollars, (2) changing raw data to percentages, and (3) converting communitywide information to a per capita format. The front-end system should also be able to make simple comparisons and utilize basic statistical techniques (Hamlin and Lyons 1993). Central tendency measures and trend line analysis on time series information should be available. A good front-end system should also be able to generate, display, and print simple statistical graphics so that the user does not always have to download information and transfer it to other software. Thematic maps should be possible in some cases.

Privacy

Privacy is both a technological question and a policy issue. The more difficult of these questions is the policy dilemma: How open should information be? Information is power. In an effective democracy we need information for both general political accountability and specific project oversight. Yet the need for personal and business privacy must be respected. These issues intensify in an economy without walls. The domain of legal users must be clearly defined for each data element.

Organizational issues intertwine with this moral and ethical question related to information. One constraint to public–private partnerships is that information collected and stored by the public remains in the public domain. Firms that are unwilling to be so open may resist entering such partnerships. Various attempts have been made to balance the need for privacy with the public demand for analysis and oversight by utilizing third-sector organizations. These quasiprivate entities have less stringent public access rules. A local economic development corporation can, for example, offer private firms more confidentiality than could a municipality. In fact, controlling access to information may be a major reason for the utilization of third-sector organizations. Defining privacy rules in advance is crucial. Otherwise, a proliferation of organizational structures becomes a way of subverting public oversight rather than of promoting public policy.

Once policy issues related to privacy are resolved (a state of affairs that will never be completely achieved), the technological question involves developing security codes that selectively restrict access to each data element by each user. This technology is advancing rapidly, but the art of cracking codes seems to almost keep pace.

These interrelated moral, legal, organizational, and technological issues are still being worked out, and represent significant challenges in an economy without walls.

Intelligent Front-End Systems

The current structure of the world economy requires better, more user-friendly software to act as the front-end system to large databases used by local planners. The front-end technology has become nearly as important as the data. It must allow access by private companies and citizens as well as government bureaucrats. This software not only should provide a simple interface but also should help the user ask the right questions before attempting to download data. It should provide the capacity for simple analysis and instant visualization. The access software needs to become an intelligent front-end system with embedded security technology. Various time series projection methods are useful basic techniques and should be built into an intelligent front-end system. These include linear and exponential time series, ratio and nested community ratio methods, and forerunner community analysis.

An example of an attempt to create an intelligent front-end system is the Economic Development Information System Project (EDIS) at Michigan State University. EDIS is an effort to create a totally self-explanatory intelligent front-end system for local economic development planners. The project is programming a set of highly user-friendly modules that carry out common economic development functions, such as feasibility analysis, time series projections, intercommunity comparisons, economic base studies, fiscal stress analysis, and feasibility analysis. The user is assisted in choosing the appropriate module based on the problem to be solved, and the modules automatically access a database for information needed to complete the analysis. Results are graphically displayed at the user's request.

PROJECTION, PREDICTION, AND ANALYSIS: THE FRONT-END SYSTEM OF THE FUTURE

In the past, urban planning tools have focused almost exclusively on extrapolating the best possible snapshot of the current situation into a similarly static view of the future. In an era of public–private partnerships, urban analysis tools must move away from reliance on single-dimensional, time series projection systems. The results of linear time series approaches are quickly outdated in a dynamic market environment. In a period of greater risk and uncertainty, planners must move toward greater use of "what if" scenario-building techniques based on simulation. "Fuzzy logic" and interval projection approaches must replace static projections. While these tools may currently be too complicated to build into the front-end system discussed above, they should be a part of the urban manager's bag of tools and a part of the intelligent front-end system of the future. This section discusses some of these concepts as they relate to the global restructuring of local economies.

Model Building

A model is a set of interconnected parameters. It is like a Tinkertoy in which each disk or node represents a set of values for a given data element, and the sticks represent relationships between parameters. The relationships take the form of functions or equations. A change in the value of one parameter directly or indirectly affects other variables in the model. One change causes the model to "operate" as the change works its way through the model. First, the values of variables connected to the initially changed element respond. These changes then cause all variables connected to them to react, and so on. In this way, we see how inputs produce outputs after passing through complex relationships between parameters.

The relationships between variables in the model (i.e., the sticks) are educated guesses. These formulas or algorithms may be based on empirical research or theoretical extrapolations from incomplete empirical studies. In these cases, the model is a predictive theory. Use of such a model produces "true" results until new empirical findings invalidate one of the supposed relationships and call the theory into question.

This kind of model attempts to be scientific, and is the primary mental paradigm for building and testing scientific theory. In an era of greater public and private interaction, much more empirical research and theory building needs to be completed in order to better understand how markets work and respond to public intervention. The importance of scientific theory building and testing remains unquestioned, yet the process moves very slowly, often too slowly to explain rapidly changing social phenomena. It also, by definition, excludes, to the extent possible, intuition or observer bias. The religion of science is objectivity.

In the fast-moving, complex social system characteristic of a market economy, reliance on traditional forms of scientific inquiry may not be fast enough. Methods need to be employed that quickly build approximation models of real systems. To do this, we need to rely less on empirical research. We need to tap the accumulated knowledge of experienced people. The intuitive understanding of experts is often the best knowledge available. It may be the only source of knowledge that can be applied quickly to build models in order to determine how complex market systems work. Making decisions using approximation models based on expert intuition obviously involves risk, yet making no decision can also be risky.

"What If" Scenarios

Models can be very simple or highly complex. One of the advantages of model building is that having a working computer model allows one to build "what if" scenarios. By labeling one of the variables in the model as an outcome, one can then test the effect of changing the value of other variables on that outcome. This allows for sensitivity testing. How sensitive is the rent for moderate cost housing, for example, to changes in the property tax millage? If one has a model that links the two directly and/or indirectly, through the sticks and disks of the Tinkertoy, one may be able to receive an approximate answer to that question.

The model also allows for dynamic forecasting. If the "what if" is not just a single change in the value of an input, but a continuous change, the model can trace the dynamic relationship between that input and the defined output. The model user may want to test more than changes in inputs. One can also test the sensitivity of changes in the sticks of the Tinkertoy. What happens when the assumed relationships between functions are altered?

Expert System

An effective front-end system should also act as an expert system. "Expert systems are computer programs that apply artificial intelligence to narrow and clearly defined problems" (Kim et al. 1990, p. 3). While the phrase "artificial intelligence" makes them seem esoteric, expert systems can be simple. As the name implies, the expert system provides knowledge in problem solving similar to that obtained by hiring an expert. In other words, in a narrowly defined repetitive task, the experience of an expert is captured and embedded in the program of steps.

Professor Edward Fergenbaum of Stanford University, an early pioneer in expert system technology, has defined an expert system as "an intelligent computer program that uses knowledge and inference procedures to solve problems that are difficult enough to require significant human expertise for their solution" (Giarratano and Riley 1989). That is, an expert system is a computer system that "emulates" the decision-making ability of a human expert.

Expert systems combine rules with facts to draw conclusions based on theories of logical deduction. The subject of an expert system is called the domain, while the collection of facts, definitions and computational procedures that apply to the domain is called the knowledge base. The set of procedures for manipulating the information in the knowledge base to reach conclusions is called the control mechanism. (Kim et al. 1990, p. 4)

For example, conclusions from a set of facts and rules of the form "If (premises), then (consequences)" can be drawn by control mechanisms, as well as procedures for determining which rules to examine first and which facts to obtain by querying the user.

Before 1980, applications for expert systems were only found in medicine and chemistry. Since then, a rush to apply them to other fields has occurred. Applications of expert systems can be described according to the problem-solving activity they perform. Several categories are interpretation, diagnosis and prescription, design and planning, monitoring and control, and instruction.

"Interpretation means inferring situation descriptions from data" (Kim et al. 1990, p. 6). One example of this type of system is used with database front-end systems. Combining expert systems with traditional databases can aid in retrieving data for subsequent analysis. Such a database could have a "front end" that incorporates the knowledge of an expert in the domain of the database in order to help users formulate queries, devise strategies for efficient searches of the database, and eliminate inconsistencies and repetitions in retrieved data. Such a system could be developed to leverage the raw information potential of a large database.

As part of the front-end system to a database, the expert system could ask a series of questions of the user. Based on the expertise of the person or persons who developed the system, conclusions would be drawn, or paths of logic followed, based on the user's responses. The user might then be told what kind of analysis to undertake or what data to access. The system might then automatically carry out a part of the analysis by accessing a local database or entering on-line into the mainframe and extracting the needed information. At this point it might ask the user additional questions, the responses to which would further refine the analysis.

One important feature that distinguishes expert systems from conventional computer programs is their transparency. In other words, the user is able to ask questions during an interactive session to learn how the program reaches a conclusion or why the program asked the user for certain information. Then, the expert system can show the chain of reasoning that was used for the outcome.

As can be assumed from the section on model building, expert system logic can also be used to build more complex models. When attempting to create the functions that describe the relationships between parameters in the model, a panel of experts can be consulted and the results of their input added to the model. While this is not an objective way to build quantitative models of complex systems, a kind of intersubjectivity emerges that can be helpful.

The intentional altering of one of these relationships creates a "what if" scenario. The model user can ask, "If this relationship is different from our expectation, what impact would a new assumption have on the outcomes of the model?"

Interval Answers

Rather than finding precise answers to quantitative questions, "fuzzy logic" provides interval answers, sometimes with probabilities associated with each point inside the interval (Skala 1988). When some operation is then performed on two interval answers (e.g., multiplied, or subtracted), the interval probability curves are interfaced. The subsequent answer is a new interval with an associated probability curve. If great uncertainty exists in the information used in the analysis (i.e., large ranges exist), interval sizes multiply as more mathematical operations are required.

On the one hand, a huge interval in the final answer gives dramatic meaning to the phrase "garbage in, garbage out." On the other hand, fuzzy logic creates a kind of simulation game environment that allows one to work in an ambience of uncertainty. By rerunning the equation iteratively and allowing random number generators to choose the best answer according to probability estimates, one can test a variety of outcomes. By selectively replacing intervals with fixed answers, one can create "what if" scenarios.

Theory Building

Because planners will be relying more heavily on market forces in the future, they must work with economists and other social scientists to build behavioral theories about how cities work in a market environment. While economists have developed elaborate price theories that work in a free market situation, few have been interested in attacking the problem of markets in an urban setting. In urban environments, externalities are more abundant, and market characteristics deviate more from the perfect competition model. This means public intervention into the market is increasingly necessary. It also implies that intervention generates unexpected secondary impacts and cross-market spillovers.

RESEARCH AND THE TESTING OF THEORY

On the one hand, current trends imply that both scholars and practitioners need to have a better understanding of market mechanisms, how they function, when they work, and when they do not work. At the same time, we must not fall into the trap of equating a free market economy with a laissez-faire economy. We must understand that an unregulated, imperfect market has the potential to cause more damage than no market at all.

We must also learn the most appropriate way to intervene in markets for the promotion of public policy. This means having both a practical and a theoretical understanding of feedback effects and secondary impacts. Clearly, the role of interprofessional and interdisciplinary research grows in this area.

CHAPTER 10

Summary and Conclusions: Public Entrepreneurs and Private Statesmen

SUMMARY OF THE CHAPTERS

One of the most important trends in urban planning and development is the increasing collaboration between the public sector and the private sector for mutual benefit. Economic systems are becoming increasingly mixed. This is particularly true at the local level and in the arena of real estate development. Innovative thinkers in both sectors have conjured up mechanisms for using private resources to promote the accomplishment of public policy and the implementation of plans while at the same time compensating investors and entrepreneurs for risking their personal and financial capital. This process has brought a greater innovation to government and greater sense of enlightened self-interest to business.

These trends are not entirely new. In the United States, where public planning has remained weak, planners have always been held inferior to the forces of the market, and have had to learn to use market forces to implement plans. The urban renewal programs of the early 1960s represented a significant test of this approach, and urban renewal authorities were important "third-sector" organizations. The tendency intensified during the economic downturn of the 1970s, and the Urban Development Action Grand program was probably the hallmark of the approach of that period. The trend accelerated shortly after 1983 in the United States. The recession in that year, the worst since the Great Depression, combined with federal budget cuts, became the mother of invention for new styles of development in the United States. Years of trial-and-error experience have proved that innovative liaisons

accomplishing both public and private goals can succeed without individuals
and organizations on either side abusing the relationship.

The term *public–private partnerships* has been popular since 1980.
Defined broadly, it describes an innovative set of activities in which the
public interest and private investment return are mutually pursued by a
variety of mixed, collaborative entities. In reality the partnership is more a
process than an organizational structure. The process of sharing risks and
managing externalities flows to the heart of the economic development
challenge and has existed for decades. The process of translating savings
into investment and directing investment where it is most needed has always
been a partnership in any society. In market-oriented economies, a guiding
principle is that governmental intervention should perfect the markets to
increase the efficiency of the allocation process.

In urban planning, the development process takes on a spatial dimension
as externalities abound. Public–private partnerships often mean governmental involvement to perfect the real estate market by mitigating urban
externalities so as to free the natural process of urban renewal and development. To manage this process and maximize benefits, we need to know
much more about how market mechanisms work, how governmental interventions affect their functioning, and what is unique about markets related
to urban and regional development.

Because of variations in culture, it is sometimes easy to describe the
differences between nations when discussing a particular issue. It is often
more difficult and more useful to look for similarities. Viewing Japan as
one example, many Japanese state that they do not have a highly developed
system of public–private partnerships, and that the concept, as practiced in
the United States, is not valid for Japan. While this may be true, part of this
belief may stem from a misconception about the nature of public–private
partnerships. As shown in this book, the concept, as defined broadly in the
United States, includes a spectrum of relationships between organizations
for the establishment and pursuit of mutual goals. It is not limited to normal
legal or financial partnerships. In reality, the Japanese system seems to
employ a variety of intersectoral processes. Third-sector organizations
abound, for example, and they seem to be used extensively. U.S. planners
can learn much about intersectoral partnerships from the way projects are
carried out in Japan.

In Eastern Europe, Hungarians are eager to learn about public–private
partnerships. Many do not realize that potentially they have one of the
world's unique examples. After the fall of communism, the new Hungarian
government was eager to decentralize. Nearly all property, previously

owned by the Communist state, was given to localities. Furthermore, the new constitution gave great flexibility to local governments to engage in entrepreneurial activities, including operating businesses, privatizing businesses, forming joint ventures with private businesses, and leasing or selling real estate. Unfortunately, local officials did not have the training or understanding to engage in innovative activities. They quickly privatized most housing at politically induced, below market prices. Now, short on revenues, they are selling off commercial property to make municipal ends meet. Little thought has been given to how public goals and private profit might be pursued simultaneously through innovative use of that property. Privatization is being carried out based on blind faith in the invisible hand of the market, with little understanding of the prerequisites of the perfect competition, free market model and the difficulty of urban development in fitting the model.

As seen in the international case studies, the tools used in public–private partnership activities vary greatly between the United States and other cultures. A major concern of U.S. corporations and developers is finance. An important incentive that the public sector can offer to leverage private action is innovative financing. Nearly all project financing in the United States is provided through private sources. Consequently, even a small public injection of equity, debt, or risk sharing can be crucial to leverage that private financing. As a result, the promise of a small public injection can be exchanged for a major alteration in project plans so as to better serve public policy objectives.

Project finance seems to be much less important for East Asian real estate developers, and therefore a less valuable negotiation item for public intervention into the real estate markets. Of critical importance to the private sector in Japan and the four dragons (Korea, Singapore, Hong Kong, and Taiwan) is the treatment of land. This may be because land is very expensive. Also, in Japan, family ownership of land is revered, and the sale or transfer of land can cause very high capital gains tax assessments and other disadvantages. A primary inducement, or incentive, that public organizations can use to guide private development toward the accomplishment of public goals is the assembly of land in ways that minimize the sale of property.

In high-density environments, a critical development problem is how to modernize infrastructure. Narrow streets, irregular lot lines, small parcel sizes, and complex ownership patterns make the readjustment and assembly of land a crucial first step in the redevelopment process. While these problems clearly exist in central city redevelopment districts in the United

States, the magnitude of the problem is different in Europe and Asia. Also, the greater willingness of local governments in the United States to use eminent domain powers reduces the relative importance of these problems in the overall development scenario.

In Japan, elaborate mechanisms (which U.S. planners might label public–private partnerships) are employed to build consensus among owners and residents of a project area. These mechanisms are used to change property lines and equitably distribute ownership so that redevelopment can proceed. An even greater use of intersectoral collaboration tools holds great promise to help promote quality urban development in many countries.

While goals and methods of public–private partnerships differ among countries, the philosophical foundations as described in this book are similar. Intersectoral partnership is a way to help build a consensus among the various actors of a development project or program. It is a way for all sectors to buy into a project in a psychological sense as well as a legal/financial sense. It offers a feeling of ownership by participants in the public goal-setting process and sensitizes all to the investment return equations faced by the private participant.

Public–private partnerships are a way for public policy to intervene in the marketplace to facilitate private-sector action that promotes public policy. The strategy attempts to use the power and skills of the private sector to accomplish public policy. Intervention typically is for the purpose of promoting development in an area that is not naturally served by the private free market.

An example of a problem that is common in several countries, albeit for different reasons, is repopulating the center of the city. In some of the central wards of Tokyo, for example, population is declining. High land costs and a change in the residential environment make housing a less desirable project for private developers. Incentives can be employed to induce developers to add a certain percentage of housing to other kinds of projects. In some secondary Japanese cities, the same hollowing-out of the gray zone surrounding the central business district that occurs in the United States is taking place. Again, public intervention into the real estate market through collaborative arrangements can be used to facilitate development and nudge private investment in that direction.

In order to ensure the success of the new order of relationships between the public sector and the private sector, a new kind of information and analysis system must exist for planning and development. More accessible information is needed by both public and private participants about one another. Information must be updated more rapidly, in order to be useful in fast-moving market environments, and each local community must know more about the outside world, since market forces move quickly around the world and affect every local community. Rather than hierarchically organized banks of data, databases must be relational. Compatible arrays of information must be juxtaposed, and data easily sorted and organized into different structures.

The ever-increasing size of databases, and the need for both public and private access, means better access systems are required. User-friendly software that acts as both an expert system and an intelligent front-end system is essential. It should help the user ask the right questions before she/he attempts to access data. It should then provide the capacity for simple analysis and instant visual illustration.

Urban planning analysis tools must move away from stiff, single-dimensional time series projection systems to greater use of "what if" scenario building based on simulation techniques. The results of linear time series approaches do not last long in the marketplace. "Fuzzy logic" and interval projection approaches must replace static projections. Analysis systems must be more multidisciplinary, because few urban subsystems operate independently in a "public choice," market-driven environment. Planners must work with economists and other social scientists to build theory about how markets work and how to intervene so as to strengthen markets and produce desired results.

The trend toward an economy without walls has significant implications for democracy, whether referring to local government in advanced democracies, Eastern Europe, or a developing nation. In elective democratic systems, the viability of the democracy depends on the effectiveness of voter oversight of elected political leaders. This in turn depends on the intelligence of the voters and the quality of the information they have. In general, the public is overwhelmed by the number of issues they face and naturally attempts to simplify choices between candidates by focusing on a limited set of issues. For an incumbent, this often means taking responsibility for a successful and visible project or program that voters can easily identify, understand, and link to the incumbent's name. Carrying out public policy by intervening in markets and establishing formal linkages with private organizations diminishes both control and identification. It reduces the credit that can be claimed for success and increases the political risks. The opposite side of the equation is that effective use of private capital can gain political allies by reducing the need to raise taxes.

Finally, economic development that utilizes complex relationships between government and companies challenges the moral and ethical fiber of both the legal and the cultural system. A greater level of trust is essential, and new forms of oversight need to evolve. Past experimentation with mixed systems illustrates that while ethical problems do arise, the challenge can also have the effect of strengthening professional ethics. These programs open up each sector to the scrutiny of the other, and induce the actors and the public at large to think about related ethical issues.

PRESCRIPTIVE CONCLUSIONS

Based on the preceding discussion and the case studies examined in this book, several important conclusions about the nature of successful intersectoral partnerships can be drawn. Some of these conclusions tend to reinforce prescriptions found throughout the existing literature on public–private partnerships, while others represent new ways of thinking about this phenomenon.

First, and in many respects foremost, intersectoral partnership should be perceived as a process rather than as merely a project or an organizational structure. This has implications for all aspects of successful interaction among the sectors. The partnership is not the completed project, itself or a one-time negotiated deal among strange bedfellows, but the total vehicle for making that project happen.This suggests that attention must be paid to the general way in which the process is approached or structured, who the partners are, how they interact, what they bring to the partnership, and how they know when they have succeeded (or failed, as the case may be). It suggests that the partnership cannot be left to serendipity, but must be carefully planned. If the process is respected in this way, the partnership has the potential to last well beyond the project for which it was originally created and/or to result in additional collaborative efforts among the partners. That is to say that successful public–private partnership is about institution building, as has been the case with HANDS in Louisville, Kentucky. It ultimately becomes a way of civic life.

Second, the pursuit of mutual goals must lie at the heart of intersectoral partnerships. The River City 21 and Sonic City cases, from Japan, both demonstrate this very effectively, though they take different paths to ensuring mutuality. Especially during the transition period, as society adjusts to the paradigm of economy without walls, we cannot automatically expect that every public–private partnership will result in an outcome that is beneficial to all with a stake. Sadly, too many examples of "partnerships" without mutuality exist, leading some to conclude that public–private partnerships are but another mechanism for deluding the public. The best way to ensure that mutual goals are diligently pursued is to involve all affected parties in the partnership process. Everyone must be "invested," whether it be emotionally, financially, or both.

Third, it should be understood that *public–private partnership* is not a monolithic concept to be carried about from place to place and superimposed on any redevelopment problem. Intersectoral collaborations must be tailored to fit the goals to be pursued. This goes back to the notion of viewing these partnerships as processes, not structures. The structure should stem from the individual process and not vice versa. The comprehensive structure of HANDS fits its goal of complete and lasting community revitalization. The Arizona Technology Incubator's structure suits its very specific goal of fostering successful high-technology businesses. Similarly, the Japanese partnerships are well suited to their focus on individual projects.

Fourth, just like any form of human organization, successful intersectoral partnerships require strong, capable leadership. This prescription is echoed throughout the literature (Fosler and Berger 1982; Porter and Sweet 1984; Levitt 1987; Daroca 1990). The leadership can come from any of the sectors represented in the partnership. In the Sonic City case, the public-sector partners took the lead. A private corporation and a state university established the Arizona Technology Incubator partnership. In the case of HANDS, it is a university that plays the leadership role, while in the case of River City 21 in Tokyo, a third-sector development corporation is the leader. As in the case of overall partnership structure, it is the goals of the partnership that should dictate the appropriate leadership.

Fifth, the role of each partner in a successful intersectoral collaboration should be clearly defined. Again, the Japanese cases stand out as the best examples of this principle. Role assignments should reflect each partner's skills, resources, and overall ability to help the partnership achieve its goals. If partners are permitted to carry out roles that are natural to them, they are more likely to do so effectively. This is not the same as saying that each partner should "do its own thing." In a good partnership, the principals must be collaborators—they must contribute to group goals while striving to meet their own needs.

Sixth, it should be understood that public–private partnerships are most appropriately used as tools for perfecting private markets. They need not be employed in instances where either the public or the private sector can achieve the goal more efficiently, effectively, and equitably. The Russell neighborhood in Louisville is a prime example of an area that is underserved by the private free market and that has problems too severe to be overcome solely by the public sector. An intersectoral partnership such as HANDS becomes the tool of choice in addressing Russell's problems.

Seventh, a new and expanded societal dialogue must take place regarding the ethical challenges presented by the economy without walls paradigm. This dialogue must be ongoing, and must balance new realities and more traditional values. We can no longer afford to ignore this paradigm shift and its accompanying ethical conundrums.

Eighth, the ways in which we collect, manage, and analyze data must be altered to meet the demands imposed by the economy without walls. Among other things, data sets must be dynamic and the flow of information among sectors must be improved. Data must be readily and easily accessible. Analysis must take place using more flexible models.

Economy without walls is a worldwide phenomenon. Will the new order be skillfully managed by public entrepreneurs and private statesmen with the collaboration of the "fourth sector," the fourth P in public–private partnership—the people (Hagiwara 1991)? Will those skills be in evidence in the local community? The answers to these questions depend on our ability to accept and understand the new paradigm and to address the issues it presents to us.

References

Ahlbrandt, Roger S., Jr., and Clyde Weaver. 1987. Public-Private Institutions and Advanced Technology Development in Southwestern Pennsylvania. *Journal of the American Planning Association*, 53,4:449–458.

Allen, David N., and Syedur Rahman. 1985. Small Business Incubators: A Positive Environment for Entrepreneurship. *Journal of Small Business Management*, 23,3:12–22.

American Planning Association. 1976. Ask Plan Landers. *Planning*, 42,4:31.

Ammer, Christine, and Dean S. Ammer. 1984. *Dictionary of Business and Economics*. New York: Free Press.

Andorka, Rudolf. 1995. Rector, University of Economic Science, Budapest, Hungary. Interviewed by Roger E. Hamlin. January.

Baldwin, John H. 1985. *Environmental Planning and Management*. Boulder, CO: Westview Press.

Bamberger, Rita J., and David W. Parham. 1984. Leveraging Amenity Infrastructure: Indianapolis's Economic Development Strategy. *Urban Land*, 43,11:12–18.

Barker, Michael (ed.). 1984. *Rebuilding America's Infrastructure: An Agenda for the 1980s*. Durham, NC: Duke University Press.

Barnekov, Timothy, Robin Boyle, and Daniel Rich. 1989. *Privatism and Urban Policy in Britain and the United States*. Oxford: Oxford University Press.

Bendick, Marc, Jr., and Mary Lou Egan. 1991. *Business Development in the Inner-City: Enterprise with Community Links*. New York: Community Development Research Center, Graduate School of Management and Urban Policy, New School for Social Research.

Bertsch, Dale F. 1984. Non-Profit Institutions and Urban Revitalization. In Paul R. Porter and David C. Sweet (eds.), *Rebuilding America's Cities: Roads to Recovery*. New Brunswick, NJ: Center for Urban Policy Research.

Birch, David. 1981. Generating New Jobs: Are Government Incentives Effective? *CUED Commentary* 3,3:3–6.

Black, Henry Campbell. 1968. *Black's Law Dictionary*. St. Paul, MN: West Publishing.

Blackford, Mansel G. 1991. Small Business in America: A Historiographic View. *Business History Review*, 65:1–26.

Blakely, Edward J. 1994. *Planning Local Economic Development: Theory and Practice*. 2nd ed. Thousand Oaks, CA: Sage Publications.

Browning, William D., and L. Hunter Lovins. 1989. *Energy Casebook*. Old Snowmass, CO: Rocky Mountain Institute.

Buccino, Gerald P. 1989. Business Failures Increasing. *Secured Lender* 45, 2:24, 26.

Buchanan, Michael R. 1983. *Real Estate Finance*. Washington, DC: American Bankers Association.

Burrus, Daniel. 1993. *Technotrends: How to Use Technology to Go Beyond Your Competition*. New York: HarperCollins.

Campbell, Candace. 1988. *Change Agents in the New Economy: Business Incubators and Economic Development*. Minneapolis, MN: Hubert H. Humphrey Institute of Public Affairs.

Capek, Stella, and John I. Gilderbloom. 1992. *Community Versus Commodity: Tenants and the American City*. Albany: State University of New York Press.

Carlson, Cynthia J., and Robert J. Duffy. 1985. Cincinnati Takes Stock of Its Vacant Land. *Planning*, 51,11:22–26.

Chae, Hee-mook. 1994. Tideland Reclamation to Reshape Inch'on. *The Korea Times*, March 31, p. 5.

Chemical Bank. 1984. Fascinating Facts About Small Business. *The CPA Journal* 54:68–69.

Choate, Pat, and Susan Walter. 1981. *America in Ruins: Beyond the Public Works Pork Barrel*. Washington, DC: Council of State Planning Agencies.

Choe, Sang-Chuel. 1993. Asian-Pacific Urban System: Towards the 21st Century—Evolving Urban System in North-East Asia. In Gill-Chin Lim and Man-Hyung Lee (eds.), *Dynamic Transformation of Societies*. Seoul: Nanam Publishing House.

Clark, James W. Julia A. Wyckoff, and Roger E. Hamlin. 1979. *Hydropower Redevelopment: A Manual Emphasizing Utilization of Employment and Training Resources*. East Lansing, MI: Proaction Institute.

Comprehensive Development Plan for the Kyongso District of Inch'on City. 1994. Inch' on, Korea: City of Inch'on.

Conway, H. McKinley, Jr., 1966. *Area Development Organizations*. Atlanta: Conway Research.

Cook, James. 1987. Priming the Urban Pump. *Forbes*, 139,6:62–64.

Cooper, Arnold C. Y. 1982. The Entrepreneurship-Small Business Interface. In Calvin A. Kent, Donald L. Sexton and Karl H. Vesper (eds.), *Encyclopedia of Entrepreneurship*. Englewood Cliffs, NJ: Prentice-Hall.

Corey, Kenneth E., Roger E. Hamlin, and Thomas S. Lyons. 1989. Non-Financial Incentives for Real Estate Development in the United States. In *Public–Private Partnerships: An Opportunity for Urban Communities*. Tokyo: Housing and Urban Development Corporation of Japan and Urban Matrix Research.

Corey, Kenneth E., and Patrick K. Kernan. 1993. Local Autonomy and Regional Development: Comparative Analyses and Information-Age Strategies for Korea. Presentation at the International Symposium on Local Autonomy and National Development in Korea, sponsored by the Korean Research Institute for Local Administration.

Dajani, Jarir S. 1978. Infrastructure Design and Impact Assessment: Bridging the Gap. In J. Eugene Grigsby III and Madelyn Glickfeld (eds.), *A Symposium on Social Impact Assessment and Human Services Planning*. Palo Alto, CA: Stanford University Press.

Daroca, Andrea. 1990. Building the Economic Development Team. In Susan G. Robinson (ed.), *Financing Growth: Who Benefits? Who Pays? And How Much?* Chicago: Government Finance Officers Association.

Davidoff, Paul. 1965. Advocacy and Pluralism in Planning. *Journal of the American Institute of Planners*, 31:596–615.

Donohoe, John P. 1988. Lollipop Condos, Air Rights, and Development Rights. *Real Estate Finance Journal*, 4,1:64–68.

Durbin, Steve. 1992. Bluegrass State Poll. *Louisville Courier-Journal*, April 27.

Eder, Peter. 1995. Assistant professor of agricultural economics, University of Agricultural Science, Godollo, Hungary. Interviewed by Roger E. Hamlin. March.

Farrell, Larry. 1986. Building Entrepreneurship: Global Perspective. *Training*, 23,7:42–50.

Flick, Frederick. 1987. Real Estate Finance Blazes New Trails. *Real Estate Today*, 20:22–26.

Fosler, R. Scott, and Renee A. Berger. 1982. *Public–Private Partnership in American Cities: Seven Case Studies*. Lexington, MA: Lexington Books.

Fulton, William. 1989. *Reaching Consensus in Land-Use Negotiations*. Planning Advisory Service Report no. 417. Chicago: American Planning Association.

Giarratano, Joseph, and Gary Riley. 1989. *Expert Systems: Principles and Programming*. Boston: PWS-KENT.

Gilderbloom, John I., Richard Appelbaum, Michael Dolny, and Peter Dreier. 1992. Sham Rent Control Research: A Further Reply. *Journal of the American Planning Association*, 58,2:220–223.

Gilderbloom, John I., Reginald Bruce, Betsy Jacobus, Maurice Jones, Mariann Kurtz, John Markham, Dan McAdams, Rob Mullins, Gloria Murray, Russ Sims, Jack Trawick, Sam Watkins, Jr., and Steve Zimmer. 1994. *How University/Community Partnerships Can Rebuild Lives and Neighborhoods, Annual Report on HANDS.* Louisville, KY: Center for Urban and Economic Research, University of Louisville.

Gilderbloom, John I., and R. L. Mullins, Jr. 1994. The University as a Partner for Rebuilding an Inner City Neighborhood. Unpublished working paper. Center for Urban and Economic Research, University of Louisville.

Gilderbloom, John I., and Mark T. Wright. 1993. Empowerment Strategies for Low-Income African American Neighborhoods. *Harvard Journal of African American Public Policy*, 2:77–95.

Gilmore, Donald R. 1960. *Developing the "Little Economies."* New York: Committee for Economic Development.

Gunyou, John. 1990. Managing Economic Development Resources. In Susan G. Robinson (ed.), *Financing Growth: Who Benefits? Who Pays? And How Much?* Chicago: Government Finance Officers Association.

Hagiwara, Schun. 1991. The Fourth Sector in New Planning. Presentation to the 1991 Annual Convention of the Japanese Planning Association. November 12.

———. 1993. Is Now the Time of Growth Management for an Ever-Growing City?: A Case Study of the Tokyo Bay Waterfront Subcenter Project. In Gill-Chin Lim and Man-Hyung Lee (eds.), *Dynamic Transformation of Societies.* Seoul: Nanam Publishing House.

Hamlin, Roger E. 1994. The Korean West Coast Development Strategy in the Pacific Rim Era. In *Proceedings of the International Seminar on the Korean West Coast Development.* Seoul: Korean Planners Association.

Hamlin, Roger E., and Thomas S. Lyons. 1989. Public–Private Partnerships for the Promotion of Real Estate Development: A Comparison of Selected Practices in the United States and Japan. In Jack Friedman (ed.), *Proceedings of the 1989 Annual Conference, San Diego, CA.* Chicago: Real Estate Educators Association.

———. 1990. Public–Private Partnerships for Urban, Regional and Economic Development. Unpublished paper presented to the Pacific Regional Science Conference Organization Summer Institute for Economic Development in the Southeast Asian Pacific Rim. Bandung Institute of Technology, Bandung, Indonesia. July.

———. 1993. Public, Private, and Nonprofit Sector Interactions for Economic Development in a Restructuring World: Implications for Professional

Planning. In Gill-Chin Lim and Man-Hyung Lee (eds.), *Dynamic Transformation of Societies*. Seoul: Nanam Publishing House.

Hamlin, Roger E., Thomas S. Lyons, and Jack H. Knott. 1990. A Policy Information and Planning Model for Urban Redevelopment Through Public–Private Partnerships. Unpublished paper presented to ELF Foundation Essay Competition.

Hamlin, Roger E., and Gail Oranchek. 1987. *Corporate Apartments*. Tokyo: Tokyu Land Corporation.

Hegedus, Jozsef, and Ivan Tosics. 1993. Hungarian Housing in Transition. In Gill-Chin Lim and Man-Hyung Lee (eds.), *Dynamic Transformation of Societies*. Seoul: Nanam Publishing House.

Hegedus, Jozsef. 1995. Interviewed by Roger E. Hamlin. January.

Holland, Robert C. 1984. The New Era in Public–Private Partnerships. In Paul R. Porter and David C. Sweet (eds.), *Rebuilding America's Cities: Roads to Recovery*. New Brunswick, NJ: Center for Urban Policy Research.

Holtzman, Samuel. 1989. *Intelligent Decision Systems*. Reading, MA: Addison-Wesley.

Housing and Urban Development Corporation of Japan. 1989. *River City 21*. Tokyo: Urban Renewal Department.

Huddleston, Jack R. 1981. Variations in Development Subsidies Under Tax Increment Financing. *Land Economics*, 57,3:373–384.

Huxhold, William E. 1991. *An Introduction to Urban Geographic Information Systems*. New York: Oxford University Press.

Hwang, Hee-Yun. 1995. Professor of urban engineering, ChungBuk National University, Korea. Interview by Roger E. Hamlin. July 26.

Jones, Oliver, and Leo Grebler. 1961. *The Secondary Mortgage Market: Its Purpose, Performance, and Potential*. Los Angeles: Real Estate Research Program, UCLA.

Juergensmeyer, Julian C. 1985. *Funding Infrastructure: Paying the Costs of Growth Through Impact Fees and Other Land Regulation Charges*. Gainesville: University of Florida Press.

Kim, T. J., L. L. Wiggins, and J. R. Wright. 1990. *Expert Systems: Applications to Urban Planning*. New York: Springer-Verlag.

Kiss, Robert. 1995. Vice president, Budapest School of Politics. Interviewed by Roger E. Hamlin. January.

Krumholz, Norman. 1984. Recovery: An Alternate View. In Paul R. Porter and David C. Sweet (eds.), *Rebuilding America's Cities: Roads to Recovery*. New Brunswick, NJ: Center for Urban Policy Research.

Krumholz, Norman, and John Forester. 1990. *Making Equity Planning Work: Leadership in the Public Sector*. Philadelphia: Temple University Press.

Landis, John D. 1990. Public/Private Development: Techniques of Project Assessment. In Susan G. Robinson (ed.), *Financing Growth: Who Benefits?*

Who Pays? And How Much? Chicago: Government Finance Officers Association.

Laughlin, James D., and Graham S. Taft. 1995. The New Act of War. *Economic Development Commentary*, 19,1:11–16.

Ledebur, Larry C. 1984. The Reagan Revolution and Beyond. In Paul R. Porter and David C. Sweet (eds.), *Rebuilding America's Cities: Roads to Recovery*. New Brunswick, NJ: Center for Urban Policy Research.

Levai, Katarin. 1995. Professor of social policy, University of Debrecen, Hungary. Interviewed by Roger E. Hamlin. January.

Levitt, Rachel (ed.). 1987. *Cities Reborn*. Washington, DC: Urban Land Institute.

Levy, John M. 1981. *Economic Development Programs for Cities, Counties, and Towns*. New York: Praeger.

————. 1988. *Contemporary Urban Planning*. Englewood Cliffs, NJ: Prentice-Hall.

Lichtenstein, Gregg A., and Thomas S. Lyons. 1996. *Incubating New Enterprises: A Guide to Successful Practice*. Washington, DC: Aspen Institute.

Logan, John, and Harvey Molotch. 1987. *Urban Fortunes: The Political Economy of Place*. Berkeley: University of California Press.

Long, Andrea L. 1984. Lecture on state economic development incentives delivered at the University of Michigan. September 25.

Louisville and Jefferson County Planning Commission. 1984. *Russell Neighborhood Plan*. Louisville, KY: The Commission.

Loewenstein, Louis K. 1978. The New York State Urban Development Corporation: A Forgotten Failure or a Precursor of the Future? *Journal of the American Institute of Planners*, 44,3:261–273.

Lowry, Ira S. 1992. Rent Control and Homelessness: The Statistical Evidence. *Journal of the American Planning Association*, 58,2:224–228.

Lueras, Leonard, and Nedra Chung (eds.). 1989. *Republic of Korea*. Singapore: APA Publications.

Lyons, Thomas S. 1987. Making State Incentives Work: The Role of the Local Development Organization in the Economic Development Process. Ph.D. diss., University of Michigan, Ann Arbor.

————. 1990. *Birthing Economic Development: How Effective Are Michigan's Business Incubators?* Athens, OH: National Business Incubation Association.

Lyons, Thomas S., and Roger E. Hamlin. 1991. *Creating an Economic Development Action Plan: A Guide for Development Professionals*. Westport, CT: Praeger.

Mahanty, Aroop K. 1980. *Intermediate Micro-economics with Applications*. New York: Academic Press.

McNulty, Robert H., Dorothy Jacobson, and Leo Penne. 1985. *The Economics of Amenity: Community Futures and Quality of Life: A Policy Guide to*

Urban Economic Development. Washington, DC: Partners for Livable Places.

Minerbi, Luciano, Peter Kakamura, Kiyoko Nitz, and Jane Yanai. 1986. *Land Readjustment: The Japanese System.* Boston: Oeljeschlager, Gunn and Haia.

Mollenkopf, John H. 1983. *The Contested City.* Princeton: Princeton University Press.

Mullin, John R., and Jeanne H. Armstrong. 1983. *Westfield Incubator Survey.* Amherst: Center for Economic Development, School of Management, University of Massachusetts.

Muth, C. Robert and Roger E. Hamlin. 1979. *Preparation for Work in a Changing Economy.* East Lansing: Michigan State University Press.

Muth, C. Robert, Roger E. Hamlin, and Paul R. Stuhmer. 1979. *Design for the Delivery of Human Resource Services.* East Lansing: Michigan State University Press.

NASDA. 1986. *Directory of Incentives for Business Investment and Development in the United States.* Washington, DC: Urban Institute Press.

NASDA, CUED, and the Urban Institute. 1983. *Directory of Incentives for Business Investment and Development in the United States: A State-by-State Guide.* Washington, DC: Urban Institute Press.

NBIA. 1990. *The State of the Business Incubation Industry 1989.* Athens, OH: National Business Incubation Association.

————. 1995. *The 1995 Directory of Incubators and Members.* Athens, OH: National Business Incubation Association.

Nelson, Arthur C., and J. Richard Recht. 1988. Inducing the Residential Land Market to Grow Timber in an Antiquated Rural Subdivision. *Journal of the American Planning Association,* 54,4:529–536.

New York Urban Development Corporation. 1988. *Annual Report.* New York: New York Urban Development Corporation.

Northrup, James L. 1986. The Land Assemblage and Development Partnership. *Real Estate Review* 16:90–93.

Nystuen, J. D., F. D. Zinn, D. Sulistyo, and R. Darmasetiawan. 1991. Computer-Aided Management Advice for Loan Programs Run by Indonesian Village Women. *World Development,* 19,12:1753–1766.

Oakey, Ray. 1984. *High Technology Small Firms: Regional Development in Britain and the United States.* New York: St. Martin's Press.

Osborne, David E., and Ted Gaebler. 1992. *Reinventing Government: How the Entrepreneurial Spirit Is Transforming the Public Sector.* Reading, MA: Addison-Wesley.

Ostrom, Vincent, and Elinor Ostrom. 1971. Public Choice: A Different Approach to the Study of Public Administration. *Public Administration Review,* 31, 2:203–216.

Peterson, Robert A., Gerald Albaum, and George Kozmetsky. 1986. The Public's Definition of Small Business. *Journal of Small Business Management*, 24:63–68.

Porter, Paul R., and David C. Sweet. 1984. Goals, Processes, and Leadership. In Paul R. Porter and David C. Sweet (eds.), *Rebuilding America's Cities: Roads to Recovery*. New Brunswick, NJ: Center for Urban Policy Research.

————. (eds.). 1984. *Rebuilding America's Cities: Roads to Recovery*. New Brunswick, NJ: Center for Urban Policy Research.

Pinchot, Gifford. 1986. *Intrapreneuring: Why You Don't Have to Leave the Corporation to Become an Entrepreneur*. New York: Perennial Library.

Rafuse, Robert W., Jr., 1991. Financing Local Government. In John N. Petersen and Dennis R. Strachota (eds.), *Local Government Finance: Concepts and Practices*. Chicago: Government Finance Officers Association.

Rice, Mark, and Jana Matthews. 1995. *Growing New Ventures—Creating New Jobs: Principles and Practices of Successful Business Incubation*. Athens, OH: National Business Incubation Association and the Ewing Marion Kauffman Foundation.

Rothwell, Roy, and Walter Zegveld. 1982. *Innovation and the Small and Medium-Sized Firm*. Boston: Kluwer-Nijhoff.

Sandstedt, Steven L. 1995. Vice president of Capital BIDCO. Interviewed by Roger E. Hamlin. July 24.

Schlefer, Jonathan. 1984. Castles in the Air. *Technology Review*, 87,5:74–75.

Schnidman, Frank. 1988. Land Readjustment. *Urban Land*, 47,2:2–6.

Sharp, Donald E. 1983. State Industrial Finance Authorities: Another Source of Term Funding. *Journal of Commercial Bank Lending*, 65,10:29–35.

Sidor, John. 1982. *State Enterprise Programs*. Washington, DC: Council of State Community Affairs Agencies.

Site Selection Handbook. 1985. Atlanta, GA: Conway Publications.

Skala, Heinz J. 1988. On Fuzzy Probability Measures. In M. M. Gupta and T. Yamakawa (eds.), *Fuzzy Logic in Knowledge-Based Systems, Decision and Control*. North-Holland, Netherlands: Elsevier Science Publishers B.V.

Solomon, Steven. 1986. *Small Business USA: The Role of Small Companies in Sparking America's Economic Transformation*. New York: Crown Publishers.

Sorkin, Donna L., Nancy B. Ferris, and James Hudak. 1986. *Strategies for Cities and Counties: A Strategic Planning Guide*. Washington, DC: Public Technology.

Spencer-Hull, Galen. 1986. *A Small Business Agenda: Trends in Global Economy*. New York: University Press of America.

Steiss, Alan W. 1975. *Local Government Finance: Capital Facility Planning and Debt Administration*. Lexington, MA: Lexington Books.

Thomas, June Manning. 1984. Redevelopment and Redistribution. In Paul R. Porter and David C. Sweet (eds.), *Rebuilding America's Cities: Roads to Recovery*. New Brunswick, NJ: Center for Urban Policy Research.

Thomsett, Michael C. 1988. *Real Estate Dictionary*. Jefferson, NC: McFarland.

Tornatzky, Louis G., Yolanda Batts, Nancy E. McCrea, Marsha L. Shook, and Louisa M. Quittman. 1996. *The Art and Craft of Technology Business Incubation: Best Practices, Strategies, and Tools from 50 Programs*. Research Triangle Park, NC: Southern Technology Council.

To'th, Elmer. 1995. Executive director, Local Enterprise Agency of Heves County, Eger, Hungary. Interviewed by Roger E. Hamlin. June 4.

U.S. Small Business Administration. 1984. *The State of Small Business*. Washington, DC: U.S. Government Printing Office.

————. 1991. *The State of Small Business*. Washington, DC: U.S. Government Printing Office.

Vaughn, Roger J. 1984. Rebuilding America: Financing Public Works in the 1980s. In Michael Barker (ed.), *Rebuilding America's Infrastructure: An Agenda for the 1980s*. Durham, NC: Duke University Press.

Vesper, Karl. 1983. *Entrepreneurship and National Policy*. Chicago: Walter Heller International Institute for Small Business Policy.

Virag, Rudolf. 1995. Deputy head, Department of Self-Government, Ministry of the Interior, Hungary. Interviewed by Roger E. Hamlin. January.

Weaver, Clyde, and Marcel Dennert. 1987. Economic Development and the Public–Private Partnership. *Journal of the American Planning Association*, 53,4:430–437.

Williams, Kristine. 1986. Business and Industrial Development Corporations (BIDCOs): An Innovative Approach to Small Business Financing. Unpublished paper.

Woodward, Colin. 1995. Hungarian Prime Minister Hits Privatization Breaks. *Christian Science Monitor*, February 1.

Yokohama City. 1987. Yokohama's Minato Mirai 21. Brochure. Yokohama, Japan: Yokohama City.

Young, Kyoo Joo. 1993. A Commentary Discussion on Urban and Regional Planning for a New Era. Unpublished paper. International Conference Inauguarating the Urban Engineering Program at Yon Sei University, Seoul, Korea.

Zorn, C. Kurt. 1991. User Charges and Fees. In John N. Petersen and Dennis R. Strachota (eds.), *Local Government Finance: Concepts and Practices*. Chicago: Government Finance Officers Association.

Index

About the Authors

ROGER E. HAMLIN is Professor of Urban and Regional Planning and Director of International Programs at Michigan State University.

THOMAS S. LYONS is Associate Professor of Urban Policy and Management at the University of Louisville.

Together, they authored *Creating an Economic Development Action Plan* (Praeger, 1991).